A Map of the Territory

Nigel Forde lives in York, where he began his career as an actor at the Theatre Royal. He co-founded Riding Lights Theatre Co., and has contributed to many BBC radio programmes, most notably as a presenter of Radio 4's *Bookshelf*. One of his screenplays for the BBC 2 animation series *Testament* won an EMMY, and his latest film was awarded a Special Distinction at the 2002 Anneçy International Animation Festival. He has written screenplays for two films, and a musical co-written with Arnold Wesker has been premiered in Japan. Nigel Forde has won a number of prizes for his poetry.

Also by Nigel Forde

Poetry
Teaching the Wind Plurals

Prose
The Lantern and the Looking Glass: Literature and Christian Belief
A Motley Wisdom: The Best of G.K. Chesterton

NIGEL FORDE

A Map of the Territory

Oxford*Poets*

CARCANET

First published in Great Britain in 2003 by
Carcanet Press Limited
Alliance House
Cross Street
Manchester M2 7AQ

A CIP catalogue record for this book is available from the British Library
ISBN 1 903039 69 X

The publisher acknowledges financial assistance from Arts Council England

Set in Monotype Garamond by XL Publishing Services, Tiverton
Printed and bound in England by SRP Ltd, Exeter

To the inheritors
Vicky, Robert, Oliver, George
Tamsin and Richard

Acknowledgements

are due to the various organisations and publications by means of which some of these poems first saw the light of day: to *The Consort*, *P.N. Review* and BBC Radio 4, to Piers Browne and John Murray in whose *Glorious Trees of Great Britain* some of the tree poems were printed. 'Tenants' was commissioned by 'The Lion's Part' for Christopher Fry's birthday celebrations in the Theatre Museum; 'Orpheus' finds its origins in a Poetry Squantum at the Hay-on-Wye Festival and a version was published in *Border Country*; 'Nothing is Wrong' won the Lace Poetry Competition and 'Visitors' a Bridport Prize. 'Movements' was published in *The Big Book of Little Poems*, ed. Roger McGough, for The National Advice Centre for Children with Reading Difficulties. As the acrostic shows, 'The Other Side of Language' was a birthday present.

Contents

There was a man in our village who could pick
A hard winter like a Derby winner; see
Its horizon creeping in early June. He'd sniff
The Great Bear, glimmering, hanging like a crane-fly
By one leg from the telephone wires; his wood stack,
Butterscotch ring on ring, was pure geometry.

His long axe opened a tree like a book,
And then he'd read it. His wet, black garden,
Pickled in horse-dung, was a barrack square.
Leeks, marrows, cabbage, lettuce and green
Potato-lanes bellowed with bees sucked
Into serfdom from the brimming hedgerows.

The seasons' pilot, he could pull down rain,
That quiet element, and send back fire
In a slow wink through marbled air like endpapers
Of a Victorian Bible. In evening light
His five-foot shadow fell twelve feet away.
He spoke seldom. We never heard him sing.

But when we needed windows, he patched nothing
With nothing more; a second sun under his fingers.

Visitors

They are building, this March, between
Eaves and rafters, somewhere in the hot dark;
Haunting the bedroom with feathered sounds.

At morning they are wingbeats in the copper beech,
Wet runes by the water bowl or shadows quietly
Bending to the business of cool gardens.

We cannot name them. Loose in the sun they sing,
But come silently, invisibly, home to roost,
To fidget like stars all night, or soft rain on stones.

Reading in bed, we listen for them now,
As for the door scrape of a daughter safely home;
They peck along the roots of our noisy dreams

In whose half-light we follow ourselves back
Along the uncertain ways of love again,
Through a frost-creak stir of silence, the tiny

Spider's footfall of an egg ticking.
The stealthy quotidian, the sift of our history
That was frail and unrehearsed; that is adequate.

Autumn Birch

All colours are precarious, but yours
Chancier than most. The sun along the hill
Yawns, and they're gone: yellow on yellow, stores
Of distances that shuffle themselves, until

The here and there are both, or neither. Eyes
Trained on summer greens draw false conclusions,
As if your branch-tips in the surly skies
Were ribs of water, merely: light's illusions

Cancelling, conceding, like the flames
Your white logs breed to tease our darknesses.
Vermilion waterfalls, the funeral games
We play to prove the world is what it is,

And that our lives go gracefully for these
UnEuclidean, mad geometries.

Capella

When you woke me and pointed to Capella swinging
From a trapeze of cloud, I remembered the wood shivering
Between me and the black wind forty years ago; and how
I ran from nothing through an orphanage of leaves; cold,
Wanting the old moon's watermark, the serenade of windows.

Day after Day

The junk and plush of the night sky gone, this air
Delivers the burnt-bacon smell of fires
Like quotations from a mother tongue.

I understand the jargon of this light
That says, exactly, what is inexact,
And goes on saying. Living wood and dead
Mingle their deep-grounded scents and shapes
With mornings, with the small, dissecting mist,
Blurred lamplight, candle-shifts; compose a text
That is maquette and scripture and lodestone
To drag the needle round the compass-card.

This is not random, this is written, fixed;
This is what clocks will leak, dreams recompose,
Some curve of harmony lean to and lose again,
And mirrors whisper of in their green goings.
The pattern slips, but it is always there.

Some chancy leap of daybreak, the bright brass
Of sun on hoarfrost, the wild, stacked-up miles
Above the trudge of clouds in sour counties
Will, all at once, collapse the artifice
Of gesture and approximation we
Have come to think becomes us. Box within box
Flies open; world on world revives. The trees
Image the kingdom we could never find,
Whose storied silence, whose world of difference
Hides, in the false sufficiency of words,
Such hunger and such habitude; such loss.

Nightingale

for Norman MacCaig

I've seen you, nightingale; not often,
And you're little to write home about.

Not like the swallows who make paisley patterns
On a scarf of sky,
Or starlings carrying violin cases,
Their hats tipped over one eye.
The fine pheasant models for *Country Life*,
The lark bounces off nothing after nothing
And then hangs from it.
And you're one of the crowd.

But then, invisibly, in the May dusk,
You open your mouth, and there's a golden riddle
To be solved. And who remembers
The yellowhammer's plainchant then?
The operatic thrush? Or the bluetit
Coming home in the back seat of the coach?

Canons and fugues are fired off
Into the darkness. There's moonlight
In your italics, curlicues: loud metaphors
Scribbled on the envious silence.

Indoors, we listen to those great composers,
Tallis, Palestrina, William Byrd.
Outside is holy ground.

Alone in your blackthorn cathedral
You're doing the impossible again: singing,
In one voice, a motet for five.
A second miracle. The first
Was when you turned
Air into wine. The third
Will happen later; indoors, and in winter.

The Visit

Arriving, you cross the lawn, brush lemon balm,
Glossing the irresolute autumn air
With footnotes of summer whose days are in retreat,
Rooted in blackthorn shadow. Tons of snow
Hang in the sky's cupboards; and we know
Where we are, but not how to repeat
The simple steps that brought us here from there.
Through the window steps a Purcell psalm:

Crushed jewels, pewter, the sinews of harmony
Anatomised, restored; all choices lost
In perfect form. Just so, the simple sense
Of knowing who we are is lost, like light
Retreating, or music's grand behaviour. White
Roses drift and flutter through the fence.
And then your voice laces the robin's: crossed
Wires, where love, nature, art agree.

I take the long path to where you wait for me;
A slow rake's progress, loving all I see.

Tenants

for Christopher Fry

That the winter could dance with such spring meanings.

I had seen bricks laid in their slick of marzipan,
Stones chafed and channelled – mere craft – and woodwork:
The sweet bite of the dovetail joint; endgrain
On silk. Stanford and Turle I had unlaced
From crumbling pages to the crumbling air.
None of their languages ever became my own,
But scattered evidence of a brief possession,
A space, a hunger for the truth of things.

This is what you defined; like Janus looking
All ways at once; x axis, y axis,
Syntax and the ache of our creation
On which you plotted lives that shaped our own.
You gave us back, polished and pure again,
All we had lost of love and truth and pain.
The background noise that clogs our telescopes
You turned to sense and innocence, with the shock
Of fat water shelled from thin, dry rock.

And all the angles of eternity
We'd stared out of existence or denied,
Suddenly glean a light, as if from water,
That puts out feelers and explores the hard
Facts of the day, the obstinate world's non-fictions,
The valley of the shadow of life, the teeth
Of whatever evidence there is. So nail
And bark and apple, mud and stone and candle,
Crocus and acorn and the rootless dew
Overflow from image into meaning.

We're tenants of a world you have in freehold,
Diving for shelter underneath your thatch
Of language. You will send us out again
Into a garden plundered by the frost,
But able, with an ability beyond
Our own small wisdoms; trailing your timely star
That lightyears through the well-bred feet and inches
We were brought up on, instinct with a fire
We cannot handle, tame or turn aside.

We bring our empty pages to your flame,
And look! They warm and blossom to a text,
The secret, invisible writing that defines
The lives we proved along your living lines.

A Lesson

This was a pond in my father's day. Dry now
For twenty years, the grass needs a greedy wind
To be water again, to shake a spray of light
Over my gaberdine and drawstring shoe-bag. Pinned

Like a picture on the morning's wall,
Light from the classroom makes its yellow claim
To be the only light. I trudge towards
A world of lists, maps, tables; answer to my name.

Beyond the playground's pasture, the free dusk
Hangs trees about me every evening; thought
Too close, too lively for these tidy rooms
Whose careful labels lie that knowledge is what's taught.

I know the night's inventions; the black winds,
The blind domestic waters in the roof-space
Soughing their dreadful tables, hissing my name
Over dry ponds. Old knowledge, this, and commonplace

As maggots in the blue reek of the badger,
Or the slab of water, spider-still, that hid
From afternoons in bracken; fat thunder-rain
That riddled the breath-hot air, stamped on the meek world's lid.

At school we have raffia and paint and glue.
The teacher's tea comes promptly in at two.

Departures

The sumac is a tinderbox; the hills
Chain smoke. Woods, bare as cloves, draw down
A tattered rigging as the light see-saws
Refusing boundaries. Skies shiver, drown
In deer-slots degged with rain. The shortened days
Are needle-eyes, and dark and winds can drive
From nowhere, raising ghosts in kindly rooms.
Cold storage. A dead language come alive.

I choose to be wordless. My dumb breath describes
Dissolving serifs on the moving air,
Ephemeral descants – gone, obeying laws
That mind and memory refuse to bear
The weight of. Shut the window. Start the car.
Cover the distance. Nothing is to spare.

A Map of the Territory

Nothing moved the day we moved; when light
Was blunted in a world without edges,
A rimless, undifferentiated white.

The sky was a load-bearing beam, the snow roof
Sagged, straining to cave in. One feather
From a robin's wing could start the avalanche.

Cramp-eyed against the glare, I sat behind
In the open lorry, watching the blue our tyres
Crimped into the snow-dunes where a road might be,

My back against the blanket-box, my legs
Lagged in gaiters and sacks. I saw cottages
Swing in a stone world from a string of smoke.

No language. Words were kidnapped by the cold.
We crawled through a speechless landscape, till the dark
Danced off the waste beyond the rodding headlamps.

Then the cellar reek of empty rooms, cold grates;
A worm on the step like a dropped pencil. We unpacked
Three plates, three cups, to tell us who we were.

A strange word, *kindling*, for the sticks on which
We brought the frost indoors. Like *dearling*,
We supposed, or *gosling* – a diminutive,

A small, kind something that we heaped against
The unkind cold on hills of moth-soft ash.
A cat-lick of crawling flame, a snap, a hiss

Unbent them in a slow, golden stretch,
Loosing the traffic of our blood and – sweet
As the slack-skinned windfalls on the kitchen floor –

Drifting in snuff and spice till even air
Was visible. As they burned, their whole life passed
Before our eyes, across the walls. A jangle

Of charcoal shadow branches, growing, waving
Noiselessly. We watched a year a second
Shiver and fade like the wintering of love.

Then tiny tickings; warm wood, cold pendulums,
The shed door creaking in a nag of wind,
And the kettle, like soft rain on the hazels.

There was an art to bringing in the ivy.
Levering its soft cable from bark-burr or frost
Took skill. It could snap like a slow worm; leave

Its tail in your hand, a piece of stiff calligraphy
Sans serif. Holly was easy. We marked out our tree
Two weeks before Christmas and we waited

For a crisp and windless morning when the sky
Was empty of even the memory of birds,
And a daylight moon melted like thin ice

On the cow-mashed clay. We went armed with knives
And whetstoned billhook. I climbed and shook in the windsway,
On the antler-toss and bamboo spring of branches;

Sliced through a needling of leaves to holly's
Sharp centre, a top-of-the-milk whiteness that seeped
Nettles and sweat, spat seeds of fire gathered

For our darkness. We noosed it in string and went
Back to a world of bacon, toast; to be
Disjoint, estranged, to make our rooms astonished.

We knew our place. There, where after dark
The echo of the light was loud enough
To ring out a trecline, to let the damp of it

Come to us, woody as viols, thinning to a treble
Sweetness, like a wake of hay on trawled
Fields; dissolving the concentrated miracle

Of earthy things stacked in our secret minds
For fingering all night like scabs or scars,
To feel the oddness of. We lay on logs,

A woodpile labyrinth of juts and angles;
Knotted, elbowed: our fakir's bed of nails
To free and mortify. We lay easy

And heard it whisper with the wild cats, nameless,
Torn-eared, sheathed like knives beneath our backs.
We let the ragged wind unspool us. Out

On its high old tide, out of the hourglass world
To drown in an amazement like the stars;
A thumb on the world's scales. Knowledgeable, sure.

The Ordnance Survey doesn't know it but
There is a field here with my great-grandfather's name;
It's hardly meadowland – rough pasture, rank nettles, elder,

And a scribe-like flourish of gothic brambles.
Hard seeds rattle here in autumn and stones stub up
out of frost-bleached grass. The clay will suck a boot off.

A gravestone of a field, exhausted, raked with weasels,
It rustles even on windless nights with fretful broodings;
It is the other side of somewhere. No one loves it;

Not as they love the bluebell wood that gleams
With water and sharp leaves, but children play here
Where beauty does not clutter them. Its negations,

Its ungroomed stubbornness, its taken-for-granted
Plainness is another kind of gift that haunts us,
Beyond the capable five senses, with the force

Of what it freed. It was here we learned that statues
Struggle from stone, that the only ease we may demand
Is the need, always, for the odds to be against us.

There's no way back to ancestors. Fathoms down,
They seem to nibble at our bait of love;
Sometimes we even imagine a twitch on the line,

But no – they will not breathe our air. We wrap it instead
Around remembered words and hand them down
Like old clothes, loved, misshapen, out of date.

Their truth, like ours, is in the habitual insignificant:
In everything forgotten: the long starings
Into the fire, the pinching out of plants,

The slow tread upstairs, the burr of frost
Along the greenhouse gutter; a glass noticed,
Wiped with a tiny window by the morning sun.

I tell my children how their great-great-grandfather drank
Paint-water instead of parsnip wine and turned
Old Testament prophet. Never how he cycled

The leaf-glued lane between the orchards. Never
How apples glowed like brake-lights in the mist,
And soft plums were bloomed like chapel slates.

Grass foamed like green sherbert at the clinking mouth
Of the plough horse. From soil, cement, straw,
Sacking, cow-cakes, the barn stung our eyes with dust.

It swung like angels, scrolled in the sunslant, dared us
To know we breathed it. Even in the clout
Of a November frost that locked the silage pools

Into amber, the littered straws into wirework,
There was always the haul of sweat and leather
To walk us, jingling, back through the short summer.

On the day the tractor came, a Fordson Major
In its soldier's immaculate blue and red, it stood
Like a prize shire, a sculpture of Energy, surrounded

By murmuring farm-hands. And it worked, though a gatepost
Never recovered from its lack of horse-sense: fields
Fell to its remote control, spun corduroy from lovat

Effortlessly. But nobody groomed it, whispered to it.
We rubbed its clogged tobacco of oil and seed down to the metal;
Took the resin to bed with us under scrubbed nails.

A triplet against four: while *Friday Night*
Is Music Night plays Strauss, the shed door bangs
At the scrag end of winter. The stairwell is packed

With fabled darkness, it echoes with cold voices
From *Journey into Space*. The moon is drastic, alien,
White as bed-linen. It has something against walls.

In the morning, though, there will be fried tomatoes;
The kitchen will stream with condensation. The spaces
Will be impossible to join. Outside, the hens

Will make perturbed noises and perform
Their headmaster's walk. Inside, my mother
Will fill her recipe book from *Woman's Own*

And shirts and slips will blister in grainy water.
The cat comes in, frost-cold, and sleeps
As if it had invented sleep. I empty myself

Into the night's footsteps, the call of the wild,
The haste of clouds and trees, and almost understand
That I am nothing yet; am to be envied.

The village is built on those who drowned here
In brass and polished oak. Something and nothing,
They root our roads, our grass whispers to them,

Their stones drink sun, their sad angels darken
In a small rain. We're on our own. They told us so
But added that there was nothing to be afraid of.

It was just the next thing, that happened to come
Last. When old Williams tipped a tractor
On his head and pulled the ditch over himself

For decency; when a late drinker fell into the spring
That oozed round beech roots and swallowed a final pint;
When old Lew took a last spit and was found

Clamped to the bus shelter by rigor mortis,
There was no shrug to the stars, no singularity.
We rest our questions now on their hard pillows,

A row of pins, a scatter of grain for St Agnes,
And we get the answers we have always got:
We had a lean hold, and what, after all, is absence?

The field is a green furnace. Summer hugs the world
To death. The slow glass of the stream tips
And slips into mere fabric, tattered as it falls;

Pats, pats, a single hornbeam leaf until we dizzy
At what such perpetuity might mean
In hammering heat, under white simmering horizons.

Hurt Hill boils silk into the sky. It will never stop.
The brambled field, the woods, have grown transparent,
Unreliable, an X-ray of the whole light-headed land

Whose birds have fallen silent, whose rabbits
Have turned to granite. This heat will bury us
In greenhouse air, ash, dust, until we char

And sift, like vampires, into the scalding sky.
We are ironed out, we are tinder, blown like glass
And thin-spun on a world we puzzle beyond patience.

We table our elements, store our green grain,
Finger the braille of what our blindness trips on
Until some weather stuns us, smacks us down.

Tenants, lessees, the adults walk on our world
With their strange names: Stemp, Larby, Vest,
Pretty, Mort and Remnant. The school register

Thirty years ago was in a foreign language.
We won't speak it; we are Randalls, Smithers,
Richards, normal names. We have purposes,

And one of these is to be unremarkable.
We stalk and stake out our demesne, part of which
Is proper utterance: password, code and talisman.

We hold our nicknames close like a marble, moon
Of gashed glass warm in the pocket; we have filled
Our five hungry senses to the brim,

Claimed all edges, turning-points; we inhabit
The hinges of day and dark, the hem of wood
And lane, own every careful change. Nothing is beautiful,

It is simply there: what is and what is of use.
We have no knowledge but our own inventions.
We possess, we store. We make things what they are.

We sing the weave of language and of stone;
Appointments of light and darkness. A psalter cracks
With the sound of a wishbone twig. A tin

Of tiny, mustard-hot Negroids passes along the stalls.
Like Zubes in school, they are medicine and allowed.
The taste of semibreves, December, shadowed angels,

Wax polish and dust burning on lampshades.
Light here is cold, keeps itself to itself. Only
From outside do the windows paint warm stories –

The flash of God's eye – on gravestones,
On the choirmaster's bicycle. Our element
Is music. Caleb Simper, Gauntlett, Ravenscroft;

The dead who live in our pure, uncertain voices,
Who undertow the habits of our logic with an art
Beyond our invention. Walking home we feel

The shift of mystery, the flick of the grasshopper
In a hollow fist. The moon at our roots; stepping
Through darkness, an exchange of music.

Walking the woods, we learn to believe in words
We have never heard of: *numinous, consecrated*;
Here is a word-hoard made flesh, the axioms

Of Keats proved on our unphilosophic pulses.
Haecceity. We stand here beyond metaphor, within it;
In the place where metaphors are made, a cool

Forge of meanings and engagements, where
Sap goes up the beeches like a lift
And boils in the invisible blue; where the ground

Goes on for ever – pitching, rolling beyond
Horizons like the sea, until the wind
Changes and it stays like that, caught solid

As if we could believe in it, translate it
Into all the languages of dislocation, the heres
And everywheres we come to year by year.

We are fugitives, stowaways in the crafty world,
But memory has landfall in these trees, this moon
Walking in a silence we have learned by heart.

An early dog has printed its Alberti bass
On the safe C major stave of Muddy Lane,
But the atonal world insists on accidentals.

Every surface shakes. This wind has known the sea
And butts the trees in memory of shingle; shifts
The grass like a tide-race, plays ducks and drakes

With an empty Capstan Full Strength packet, dries
Our black wellingtons to a smeared ochre. When
You are in it, the lane goes nowhere much;

Nothing up the day's sleeve. No. But we bring home
More than the brittle jigsaws our boots drop
On the doormat. A prickle on the neck. The pattern

Of all that will not be patterned; the knowledge
Of something always at our shoulder; the memory
Of cold sky in rutted puddles; a mirror of clouds,

Branches, birds: tiny mud-smoked fathoms
Where the world goes round appalling, impossible corners
And on and on for ever; a trouble to our dreams.

Another dusk like snow settles. A tremolando
In the woods shakes out rooks, and spiders' webs
Of what will soon be dark. The kettle boils

And moths yearn at the window-glass for something
Of August that is in our fires. An owl
Hangs on his own words. Hearthrugged with a book,

I wonder who goes there and what I am;
What's in my head of inherited verbs and nouns;
The traffic of the past, the negotiable currencies

Of fact, fiction and memories of memories
Which seem only another way of encoding
What I already possess; the daily flavours

That met me somewhere and became me. Time
Is not. There are moths, owl, me, the fire.
Nothing is difficult, but simply awaits discovery.

Love and language I learn from both ends; each end
Of daylight, impulse and intention. There is nothing
To ignore, to dismay, to wish might be otherwise.

I must have watched its every move. The shape
On the airwaves made by the mere words
Whittall's Field, casually spoken, is fiction-sharp,

Bone and bread, earth and air, once and forever
Behind time and Time itself; the slipstream
Of all the ways we went; the mind's eye

Of each inherited landscape. Here the first trees
And the last to turn in autumn. Boot-bright chestnuts
In a wreck of shell; the unpaintable colours

Where larch stops being larch and is the air again;
The lie of the horizon, kept at the distance it's invented by.
The crunch of winter grass, the trampoline of stars;

And warm cow-flanks, and turned earth and the first myrrh
Of a cottage fire spitting out its old rain.
I snag my mind against these sweet, pain-filled

Cadences: the iron-in-velvet false relations,
The sour clash of sharp and natural,
The counterpoint of what is. What ideally is.

The bus is too big and too fast. Swaying, rattling,
Glowing in the dark like a liner. We grip
The throbbing seat-backs, breathe the bitter fabric,

Stale cigarette smoke and the cream of diesel.
The tyres sling us their impeded speech;
Branches thrash the roof, and when we peer

To watch the scattered cottages swing towards us,
Moths to the candle, and away again, we see
Our grimy selves in parallel; blurred ghosts

Hurtling beside us, sliced through by beech
And whipped by hazel. Wissick, sauntering home
With his billhook, melts into me and is gone;

A hedge switchbacks through my chest, three cows
Orbit my head, holly, painlessly, slaps my face.
Something is mocking, sifting me. The real

Out there or the real in here? I can sit for ever
Between the two, imagining the truth of either,
Imagining, even, that I need to choose.

Débâcle. The crack of thaw and the ripe sound
Of snow slithering into its own lap.
The village is crazy with bicycles and children,

A dance of dogs and a crunch of stubbled ice.
And the paper-tearing wind at last has lodged
Somewhere in branches emerging from their ghosts.

The time is always morning until darkness
Falls through the bric-a-brac of wood and cloud,
Loosening the logic of the tidy day

To what we make of what light leaves behind
Our eyes, our doors. Fires are holy, we bend to them;
Curtains are drawn and the radio ticks to the clock,

Or the piano tugs at emotions it can't define.
Outside, a bucket puts a skin across three stars.
We light our lamps, illumine our small,

Shabby histories while starlings soak
Into the hedge with a noise that says how much
There is of everything and how it matters.

Paintings. Such noisy fictions; all those old
Dutch Masters, whose whole-of-human-life
Is so relentlessly there. But fold
The family album page: one man, one wife,
In sepia silence stand against the cold
And wartime Grayswood sky, as if this were
Not a beginning but an end. We share
That changed and changeless landscape with their past;
No question – as with flowers – 'Will they last?'

Twelve curling pictures of a wedding day;
The panto cast in nineteen sixty-one;
And young Chris with a pitchfork on the hay.
Random meanings, episodes long gone
Which you contain like lines within a play
But cannot be defined by. What they show
Is an experimental section through
The family tree – a metaphor that brings
Its own image of living, golden rings.

Time somersaults in these stillnesses. One page
Mocks up a father not as old as I,
A mother yet to be my daughter's age.
Black and white fictions I invent you by,
Then match to memories the camera cannot gauge:
A tick of needles; the blue, Saturn rings
Of Condor Sliced; the safe shape of nights
When music downstairs, like a distant shore,
Slid minims, flotsam, through the bedroom floor.

The clock bangs on about time; and all we knew –
The yearly winter weight of snow on trees,
The tongues that we were taught, the maps we drew –
No longer seem sufficient strategies.
Not photographs but life alone will do;
The fire refines us in the lives we share.
Grey skies and frost you kindled with your flame
And found, in winter, for a summer reason,
This gold, this love. Sweet fruit out of season.

Making the Herb Garden

I have become acquainted with roots.
Fusewire, string, cotton, whipcord, gut and
The yellow chicken-feet of nettles:
Random geometry; the drowned miles
We never see; the power lines that
Crackle into the pure speech of flowers.

Disconnecting them from the soil's grid
Is profitless – they will web again
And haul themselves through a rockface. All
I can do is bolt the Augean
Stable-door; rip, hack, sieve, slice out the
Mauvish gold-in-blue of railway clay

And offer, like a litany, herbs
Whose names I pull across my palm and
Through my fingers like a string of beads
Homely and precious; rosemary and
Rue, borage, marjoram, sage, self-heal,
Bergamot, comfrey, feverfew. They

Lift and simmer in the slow places,
Finch-green and olive, loading the soft
Wagons of the bees, dredging oils from
Sunlight to bruise moons, to be winter
Fire. For completeness, for healing, and
The continuity of gardens.

Railway Crossing

Heat shook above the blue rails wet with sun
Under the blue sky; and the mares' tails,
Willowherb, cow-parsley, grew an inch

Higher than the heat that pricked like ants
On skin and schoolboy hair; higher by feet
Than the greased sleepers bedded on graveyard chips.

Slugged by the sun, dazed and daring we lay
Heads down in the crushed grass of the rabbit-run,
Our pennies on the rail. When ovens opened

It was the 3.04 crumbling the air in our ears,
Ramming embankment into our chests. We saw
Its wrong-end, nodding, caterpillar face,

Its backward grin. Our pennies peeled from the track,
Tongued and grooved, spent and seashell thin
But recognisable. As was the name

Of one who laid his face along the same
Smooth rails fourteen years later. Alone, afraid.
One thin, shapeless coin locked in his hand.

'Now what shall we play?' he'd said once; hid the coin.
'I'll keep that one safe for a rainy day.'
We spent thick threepenny bits on wine-gums, Tizer.

Yew

The haul of the graveyard; a bitter green
That cuts back to nothing –
   A bareness that we know in our bones.

We bring you our dead for sheltering, try
Not to think how your roots fasten
   On the undertow of earth to earth.

Your scythe of shadow mows daffodils,
Daisies. Anthems and rain and fieldfares
   Go begging by like mutes.

'Also Margaret, his wife': you are her resurrection,
Her winter voice drowned by bells,
   Furred by the slow syllables of frost.

She sings in your wires, steps through
Your branches noiselessly. For grief or hope?
   Along the wall, black cars herd and wait.

Looking into the Pond

Afterwards we could see water and the stalks vaulting its crypt.
But first (the cup or the faces?) we saw our own green shapes:
A wag of grimy glass, and there we were. Weren't. Were;
Slapped on the skin of the pond, a cut-out of intestines, a collage
Of weeds gracefully going nowhere, while the clouds
Went nowhere else another way behind our shoulders.
Swallowed down, drowned without a ripple. Much we understood;

We could get our tongues round a world that was nouns and verbs,
A simple syntax of cause and effect. Not always at night
When, beyond the churchyard wall, the bull stamped in a field
Of stones and suicides; or the unreasonable moon slung
Mercury along the garden floor; or the soft seaside air
Was starched by the lighthouse. But by day. And now the day
Was waiting to decode our familiar texts. A ruffle of wind

And Mr Clegg swung his white net like a Jersey's muslin udder
Tapering into glass; he scored a neat bullseye every time
In the big ripples, pulled out the nothing the pond had painted us on;
A tubeful that shaved the sun and spun it through our eyes.
And then the microscope, with one snatch, loosed our referents.
                                                        Free fall.
Look! what had been pure silence to the eyes, was swarming with
                                                        punctuation,
Translucent commas, full-stops, dashes. Exclamation marks

Swam on the slide, bowed, kicked, cometed in an unangelic dance
Of pinhead monsters a million times smaller than their names.
Going home, we felt ourselves spread thin, mislaid, undone,
The pond in our mouths and ears. We gagged on impossible plurals.
Nothing was trustworthy. The rules had changed. Clocks and graves
And mirrors waited to teem like water. How could we dare breathe
In a world where now the air might crawl, pounce and duck us
                                                        under?

Movements

The snow is word perfect in a hundred different silences;
Steels itself for the soundless porcelain of an early moon.
And over locked lakes, barnyard, copse, come the unhindered birds,
Strange winter fruit, lending weight to bare branches.

The Other Side of Language

T he other side of language, where you live,
O utwits our syntax, is the shape of yours.

P oems you gave us now define our lives;
E xpress with such a casual clarity
T he loves, the fears, the things we could not bear –
E xcept you chose the words – or never thought
R emarkable until you made them so.

S ixty times this month has proved itself
C apable of summer; the dark trees
U nflesh to skeletons and bloom on glass,
P ersuading white frost to green prophecies.
H ours load the clock hands; now the days grow long
A nd their enticing images breed wild
M usic, and a process; weather, light.

O n every intersection of the past
N ew futures hinge, new powers gathering

H oist out their flags. The secrets of the dusk
I nvite complicity; stars open claws,
S hake meanings down and drop them in your path

B etween the colours metaphor alone
I nvents from day's necessities. How sky
R esolves to speech, or manuscripts of moon
T rip off the tongue and roost in the mind's eye,
H ides in the grace of doing. That's your grace –
D ismantling us; glossing the world's texts
A nd ambiguities. 'Out Late', but still
Y oung in this feast and sixty winters' ends.

Figurations

At sunset, suddenly.
This calculating world was textbook plain.

Across the areas of the sky,
Four geese, in series, plotted a line AB;

Distance divided itself by a multiple of tree
Fired vectors of swifts
Between the parabolic bats.

The sun, narrowing its angle,
Multiplied radiance, subtracted radians.
Slowly, the tangent hill became a chord,
Then a diameter.

Gnats plus gnats plus gnats
Complicated their fast ellipses:
A working model of atoms.

My congruent, my similar,
My simultaneous girl,
Pure as mathematics are pure, I saw you then
As my supplementary angle; or
External to me, but the sum
Of my two opposite interiors,
Forgetting that nothing ever truly equals
Something else;
And that my poor theorem's only proved
Squarely on your hypotenuse.

Reflections

A flower's colour is the least
Of its possessions;
I see a shape rejecting sunlight
And call it bronze chrysanthemum,
Which is to know it
By the light it has refused.

The speedwell takes sunlight
To its heart, but spits out blue;
The primrose finds no use
For yellow. The violet
Is everything but violet, the pinks
Are leaking all the pink they aren't.

I still take appearances for reality,
But remember the imprecision of light's language
Brought up against the syntax
Of a single flower. I intercept
All that return-to-sender, all
The unwanted luggage of light

And use it to illumine you,
Telling myself that even your refusals
Are beautiful; that I know you only
By what you reflect; that I will not unfold
Petal after petal. I'd drown
In your deep, chromatic secrecies.

Change of Address

for Richard Stilgoe

You showed me the trees, limbs of the fading light,
Planted for music you would never hear;
Maple and sycamore and pearwood add
A ledger-line of leafage, year by year;
Drawing on moonlight, gathering, in ring
On ring, a counterpoint too subtle for the ear

Composed of raindrop, heartbeat, footfall, breath;
Tiny, unheard, domestic sounds. I stood
At the high window after you had gone,
And watched the acoustic world becoming wood:
Soundboard and lute-rose, scroll and fret and frame,
To voice the verbless language chanted by our blood.

Last year you sent a card: Change of Address.
And I thought, first, of those trees; if the new
Possessors of the house would hear the singing
Locked in the sap, the dumb fugues driving through.
Or would they rip the heart out of the silence
For more of morning light, or space, or barbecue?

Tacet. The music stalls. The trees, fallen,
Out of earshot now, curl parchment skins
From chilly trunks that wait for rot, for firesmoke
To shape on air their hundred unshaped violins.

Medlar

Fooled by window-glass, Medusa of the garden,
  The one-eyed fruit has turned itself to stone.
Five lashes point, stiffened by more than frost
  In more than silence. Rind compacts to bone;
The tongues are stilled, rose-hips shrink and harden
    A whisper of Pentecost.

But there is something still of fire in the twist
  Of trunk and branch whose cadences the mind
Raids for a memory; witch or Minotaur,
  Or something that we thought we'd left behind
In storybooks, but comes back with the mist
    As more than metaphor.

We have to look, but do not want to see the chin,
  The horrid hair, the all-too-likely clutch
Of what the medlar has instead of claws;
  The bletted fruit that slackens at the touch
Of any weather now. The rot sets in.
    We turn our eyes indoors.

Touchstones

The dark comes down, the year is behind bars;
A leave-taking, a tactical retreat
Too sudden for our tidy calendars
That clone the months, parcel the days, repeat

The yearlong litany of time doled out.
This is a dark that counter-tenor owls
Explain in code; that moonlight lies about,
That bumps domestic ghosts on chimney cowls.

Now comes the need to trace the rumour back;
Rehearse intentions for a history
We did not choose, a chain of chance whose slack
Is taken up and lugs the memory

Into the magic wood. Where memory fails,
The bones of trees whisper their winter's tales.

The bones of trees whisper their winter's tales
To solitaries, children and the dead
Named on white walls where honeysuckle trails,
Blunt-fingered, unhandy; where the window-lead

Crawls like a snake through English Galilees:
Oak-leaved, persimmoned, swans upon the lake,
Kentish apples kindling in the trees.
An everywhere made local for my sake.

Our dead lie outside like complaisant, fond
Uncles in seaside sand, buried till tea.
The sky's a drowning-pool and I'm beyond
The solace of symbol or chance imagery;

But snowdrops, fragile, bend in rain-green jars.
A thickening air is eaten through by stars.

A thickening air is eaten through by stars;
Black gutters clamp the expanding universe
Of ice, and trap a fossil Saturn. Fires
Are painted fires. Quiet hackles of grass

Rise to the frost, white iron-filings. The idea
Of coldness which is more than cold. The spider
Hangs in the coalhouse on a chandelier;
The movement of twilight quickens to its coda.

The winter smell of bread and sage and spice
Is the smell of the sky by long association;
A proxy myrrh salves gardens locked in ice;
The world is stopped down to its constellations.

We name them, number them, in our rituals:
The Twins, the Bull, the Hunter and the Scales.

The Twins, the Bull, the Hunter and the Scales:
Short fictions in the storytelling sky
That make heraldic the slow, vacant reels,
The endless roar of nothing roaring by.

Too much for us. We slip through our own fingers
Without a tale for all that is elsewhere,
Unearthly, other. With unguessed-at hungers
The sharp sky leans on fathoms of our fear.

So we domesticate; make a fireside
Of these cold burnings, a childish join-the-dots
That fakes a pattern we can dare to read
And make a small world of. Above the copse

The sauntering moon rusts in its lonely ring.
The iron age is battening down the spring.

The iron age is battening down the spring,
Staunching the leaks of green into the grey
Of morning fields or skies at evening
When coaldust swirls of starlings turn pipeclay

To marble; where the stiffening pond creaks, creased
In its winter coat. Love is less negligent
In these short days of fast before the feast,
When fires bestow what scrawny summer lent:

The pull to the centre, the informing myth
Beyond the truths we'd settled for, behind
The careful certainties we're burdened with.
Good weather, like good fortune, is unkind.

Snow's arguments confound our black and white,
Quickening dreams and stripping down the light.

Quickening dreams and stripping down the light
Until the light is nothing more than dream's
Bare metal – that's December's mode; that's night
For day, a silence for the voice of streams

And, for the voice of birds, a small, spare song,
A mere quotation remembered from July.
What moves us most is memories proving wrong
And potent by misapprehension. Dry

Logs that smell of grain stores or the guts
Of harpsichords; a scatter of cow-parsley
That is not frost. The open atlas shuts
And is a moth. The beeches stir like scree.

Nothing's substantial. Mist; an underwing;
Mapmaker's colours; a brief dismantling.

Mapmaker's colours; a brief dismantling
Of time and all the minds it's out of. Death,
That big word, is the living weight we bring
To love that sifted, voiceless, on a breath

That haunts us still, and haunts the ghosts themselves,
Murmuring in the room; a reticence
More than a presence. Fire-tongs, clock and shelves
Of unread books, a vase. The eloquence

Of things that cannot speak. They still pronounce,
Sentence by sentence, brooding imperatives
That adumbrate the present tense accounts
Our lives are written in. A small snow sieves

Between the trees these good ghosts set upright.
Now old agendas repossess the night.

Now old agendas repossess the night
And keep us from our sleep. We look for ways
To be amended, to unload the freight
Of knowing into words; as if the size

Of all the meanings we were party to –
Implicit, proxy, glad and bitter-sweet –
Could be compacted into 'yes' or 'no',
Pinned on a page; handed on a plate.

We live in the spaces between word and word,
Are outmanoeuvred by the alphabet
Which we know better than, but can't afford
To do without. Words, like Schrödinger's Cat,

Live until we look and are resigned:
The gestures of language are partial and unkind.

The gestures of language are partial and unkind,
Have only our memory as guarantees
That they refer to what we understand
By moon and trees when we say 'moon' and 'trees'.

Music. That's slippery too; self-referential,
Combining its twelve elements like snow,
Empty of everything but pure potential,
Shaping itself to what we think we know.

And that's a world for which words were invented;
Never enough to outflank the mystery,
But to be music, snowfall, softly printed;
A fictive truth we call reality

By a logic that it taught us. And we've heard
The rhyme of unreason locked in every word.

The rhyme of unreason, locked in every word
We speak, is our excuse for silence. That,
Or something simpler that the silence slurred
Then leached into our ragged habitat

Of loose-leaf winters, deftly handling
The windfall subtleties of pen and ink
And wash that dark and light at odds will bring.
Candle-parings, tithes to what we think

Is gone, enacted, will not come again
Until we trip on dreams or catch the scent
Of some thrifty warmth that wrinkles Charles's Wain
And Cassiopeia. That's all meaning meant

And will mean when the future's left behind:
A past to prove the temper of the mind.

A past to prove the temper of the mind
Is process and a vision; we explore
The legacy, cradle all that we intend
In all that brought us, lovingly, this far,

That bears our weight. Each moon holds something up
As an example. Each candle in the tree
Leaps lightly on its shadow. Wax and sap
Distil the flavour of their ancestry

Till the here and now become the now and then,
The counterpoise of entropy we keep
To turn our heads to home through furious rain,
To be the touchstone of the lives we shape.

Winters pile up behind us, dense, and stored
With metaphors, precious, potent and absurd.

With metaphors, precious, potent and absurd,
We measure the subtext, the low tricks of time,
Its obstinate motives; and, by sleight of word,
Revoke its sentences, scratch out its name.

Imagine. That greaseproof sky, that cuff of mist –
The creep, the tideline of the coming snow –
Wreathed itself, just so, about the wrist
Of the same holly a hundred years ago

And will next year. The fabric stays the same:
The stonewall of the hill at dusk, the white
Behaviour of distance, and the perfect seam
Of ice on twigs. The world and we repeat:

We question and regret, we dream and grow,
While through the dark our footsore futures go.

While through the dark our footsore futures go,
We comfort ourselves with nightlights, memories;
Falsified, placatory, we know,
And, like us, harnessed to the dead who freeze

Not in earth, but in their kind disguise
As tutelary spirits; who possess
The rooms, the reasons that we try for size
And grow to feel are ours. More or less.

Firewood, kettle, candles ghosted green
In smoky mirrors, still are ways to shape
The ends of winter to our own. The lean
Of dark condensing, steel of the landscape

That glitters, shifts and slips its chains as though
Mile upon mile is softening to the snow.

Mile upon mile is softening to the snow:
White inches over which the church bell slings
A ringing gunshot. Fox tracks, deer spoor; slow
Motion of the sky spins webs and wings,

Clots a snagged tractor to a pillow. Wind
Will carve it to a scapula by noon
And every autumn colour come unpinned
Leaving a stare, outlandish as the moon;

A naked land, a lucid, birdless sky.
Walking home along the thickening hill,
I leave my own italic spoor: *I, I*
It spells obliquely. Adam. Judas. Small

In this huge house of myths. Out go the stars;
The dark comes down, the year is behind bars.

The dark comes down, the year is behind bars.
The bones of trees whisper their winter's tales,
A thickening air is eaten through by stars:
The Twins, the Bull, the Hunter and the Scales.

The iron age is battening down the spring,
Quickening dreams and stripping down the light
Mapmaker's colours; a brief dismantling.
Now old agendas repossess the night.

The gestures of language are partial and unkind:
The rhyme of unreason locked in every word.
A past to prove the temper of the mind
With metaphors, precious, potent and absurd.

While through the dark our footsore futures go,
Mile upon mile is softening to the snow.

A Dutch Interior

The endless navigations of the day,
Simple as salt. On cucumber-cold tiles
The child kneels, his head in his mother's hands.
An attitude of blessing, or farewell?
A prayer? A nightmare banishment? All this;
Besides the weekly search for lice. There is
A door, a window, always; something beyond.
Though never, we guess, Renaissance allegory:
No Mars and Venus, no St Anthony,
No Milky Way straightlacing from Hera's curves;
An absence of dragons. Truth, in fine, is proved
Where universals shrink and are behaviour –
The unemphatic tilting of a jug,
The curl of an apple paring; where the plain
Maidservant, or the woman of the house,
Is carefully performing something humble.
She fills a glass or turns a page of music,
Smooths bedlinen; as if eternity
Were loaded with unsafe minutes, where regret
And love have to be harboured in the grace
And daily, patient gravity of doing.

Dark mirrors gloss the harmony of rooms
And cheat perspective's cheat with a dimension
Beyond the logic of interiors.
Through glass, or through a door and then a door,
A tiny world is theatred in sunlight;
The world of errands, visitors and morning
On warm Delft bricks, and sweet-faced dogs, and weeds
In perfect paving. This will pass. The balance
Is here in poised reflection, timber-grain
Worn smooth, and latticed glass, and space enough
To sigh and sleep and fold and peel and know,
In work well-ordered, the sure counterpoint
Of wholesome lives, the almost unremarked
Ache of what goes on and on and on.

Following Darkness

Within a thousand days the dream was broken,
The fairies gone to another part of the wood;
The nine men's morris all filled up with mud,
The herds diseased. A year to fatten crows.

Hermia and Lysander stayed together –
Measuring out their length on this cold bed –
For the sake of the children. Egeus sulked and said
How much the eldest looked like Helena's ex.

The Palace was opened, Philostrate served teas;
Bald Theseus gave his usual address
('Love, Lunacy and Free Verse') to the press.
Tourists bought postcards of the famous girdle.

Hippolyta, bored, drooped in white passageways;
Or in the night, awake and in despair,
How easy was her bush surprised and bare
To Demetrius's beer-gut. Bottom went

To front a TV quiz show. Quince alone
Set out for Puck roast crabs and cream each night;
Took the ensuing graces as his right,
Lived two more years and died in bed, a Tory.

But then his son, one chill midsummer's eve,
Found in the roof-space, snug beneath a beam,
Moth'd, cobwebbed, moonshined like an attic dream,
A canvas headpiece, lantern, script and sword.

A tiny music leaning on the night
Touched him with hot ice, wondrous strange snow,
As if there were no journeys left to go,
No darkness that had not been spilled by light.

Christmas Eve

In the yard, on the oldest night of the year.
The apples in my arms are robbed of scent.
From tailor's chalk the second stars appear,
As hard as nails. The stream water went

Yesterday; it turned to its own roof, a white
Whispering gallery printed by the feet
Of thrushes, brushed by their wings. There's talk of light
Behind the window. Candle and fireplace cheat

The ultramarine swoop and the rusted flowers
Whose greens bleed on the fingers. Painted snows,
Holly, carols confide. This evening loads

Us with every Christmas past; empowers
The silences with all that silence knows:
Love, like our darkness, in a million modes.

Seven Last Words

for Carl Dolmetsch

Whose cold ivory and long-dead boxwood
    Bloomed round a thread of breath and put out leaf
That glimmered green as water at the thaw,
    Conferred more meaning and a swifter grief
        Than mind had language for.

We walk, for him, in absent-minded rooms,
    Where varnished woods picked clean by silence are
Fasting on noises merely – music's slang –
    And only chill sunlight leans and learns 'L'Art
        De Toucher Le Clavecin'.

We hear, for him, the sounds we never noticed:
    The broken consorts of domestic gardens
After migration, sad and sharp and clear;
    The light that softens and the drift that hardens
        Into another year.

As if our lives were sudden dispensations,
    Considered, transformed, granted on condition,
That nothing may tidy up, nothing console,
    Only the Cana sleight of the musician,
        A holiness making whole,

Inventing places for the sifted spirit
    To find its measure. How can abstract art
(Such ghosts, such winterings, such near and far)
    Lead, like a local road we've learned by heart,
        To where all centres are?

The age-old pains we heaped on music's shoulders,
    'When I Am Laid in Earth', 'The Lamentations',
'Sehnsucht', 'Ruht Wohl', those dark, eternal aches,
    Become the pain we bear. The constellations
        Wheel kindly for our sakes,

So say our small, pathetic fallacies.
But, out of the kindly dark, the ancient light
Of stars that shone for Bach and Biber will
Come thrifty through a penetrable night;
Illuminate us still.

Lombardy Poplars

Morning drains away the ash-white
Hundred-year-old twilight;
The river, spooled by blades,
Is all surface under the light
Leap of a boat from its shadow
To its shadow, shaking
The wet stars.
Lombardy poplars and a juggle
Of darknesses; a stir of silence
And a safe day breaking
As eight backs bend
And fire for the perfect centre
Of a bridge-arch meeting water
In a perfect O.
The leaves lift with a regretful sound:
As if, as if. As if
At Cambrai, Arras, Amiens, Bapaume,
The Lombardy poplars
Might have showered some safe
Sunlight down;
And out they'd shoot,
Those blunted limbs
And smashed spaces
On short lease, once, to lovers
Of farms at harvest time and girls;
And trees that in French mud
Spoke English. Out they'd shoot,
Whole again and young
And on the Ouse,
Where now the oarsmen slump
Like shot sentries, and the boat
Slides towards breakfast, slides
Across the long, troubled ghosts
Of Lombardy poplars.

The Law of Diminishing Departures

I make tea from the water that you boiled
Before you left; use your special cup.
I choose this book because you read it last.
The fire I've kept in for days: these flames
Are still the ones you saw. The milk jug? Stet,
Because you left it there. I fool myself
With charms, connections, that should make you real
But punch your absence into every act.

I keep things too long; candles I won't burn,
Logs, ditto, saved for feasts or rainy days;
The chances are tomorrow could be worse.
And now it is. I've kept you long enough.
I study to enjoy the chilly space
That closes round my hand instead of yours,
And walk on grass to watch the rising moon
Because you might be watching too. Because.

Nothing is Wrong

I tiptoe along the unlit corridor
Where the books tick like a storm brewing.

Sleep stumbles from me; warm dreams melt
In the bed I have left. I must bring comfort now,
Not take it. Your door, half-open, shows
The cot in silhouette against the window.

Nothing is wrong. We both breathe easily;
But I feel the night's weight on me and in me.

I want my hand to be water for you; stoop
To the crumpled sheet; and then you move,
Twist, with a sudden purpose and the quick snuffle
That woke me.
        The moonlight lies: your reach
Is miles, not inches. New dimensions bend
From where you lie, and constellations gather
Unquestioningly to receive this four-week nova.

Nothing is wrong. Sound stops. The grain of the world
Runs counter; the darkness bristles with light beyond

This thin skin of window-glass. Then it's done.
Orion streams over the shoulder of the hill
And, leisurely, as if it were demanded,
You lift a hand and dip it in the stars,

Trapping vast light years in a fist of flesh;
The universe all eyes. Suddenly vulnerable.

Overnight

An hour before dark
You showed me the raw stars,
High as harmonics.

I named them
Until morning, with a small
Scrupulous frost,

Fleshed out a roe-deer
In a smoke of breath,
Head down. Still.

Puzzling out the Arabic
Of a dog-skid.

A Shadow Fugue

Cold shadows, too far flung. A sense of light
Blows like litter through the window, falls
In uninviting plainness on plain rooms
We've grown accustomed to. Unsheltered walls
Rugged with ice like candlewax, blackhearted,
Tick, purr and splatter. That grave-goose,
The water-table, shrugs beneath the land,
Hardens its arteries. The year hangs loose

To winds that creak, lament, in vocalises
For angels that announce the end of time,
Or score a thin pavane for ghosts shrugged out
Of anecdotal pasts. A game, a crime,
Who knows? Not won or solved, but reinvented
To be the homework of each generation,
Trespassers on their own lands which the dead
Still occupy with nightly perturbation.

We are perplexed inheritors whose bad dreams
Founder on good ones; the tune we want to find
Is hidden in counterpoint; even furniture
Is serious stuff and histories hide behind
It, obscurely – needing footnotes which
Are not provided. Stars dribble down the slates
And spider on the greenhouse glass. A code
Again, but repetition makes it rich

In aggregates of meaning. And that's just
What's missing from our cupboards that spill out
Their skeletons of tinsel, glass or bone
In mysterious geometries. We set about
Our temporary expedients once again,
As if what is unknown were unfulfilled;
As if the story so far were forgotten:
We trap some darkness every time we build.

Balsam Poplar

No epiphanies at 5 Crick Road. A damp room,
A greatcoat and a borrowed clavichord,
A two-bar electric fire and *The Woodlanders*.

But one morning I crossed The Parks –
Fitzpiers to the life – for a tutorial,
And scented the Balsam Poplar.
                            And I was Giles Winterbourne,
I was Marty; I was old Melbury, troubled
By the beauty he'd been given.
                        Just the Balsam Poplar,
Slow but sudden, like a bruise. You could find it
Blindfold – the best way on a morning when the mist
Has ducks' legs and a roof of sun and thrushes;
Where any tree could be any tree, and I
Was the first one across the wet grass,
Head down among the Metaphysical Poets.

It was the shape of every memory, in translation,
And unique as wallflowers; it gathered in
Old knowledge and new necessity.

That one morning spliced the Balsam Poplar
For ever with the century in my head. It is
The bracelet of bright hair, the spider,
Love, that transubstantiates all;
It is Rest in the bottom of the glass; the infancy
Of this sublime and celestial greatness.

Plane Trees in the Minster Garden

In autumn, tabby; goldsmith's work and struck
Fire. Then, in the green days, hoisted
Into a clarity of air on endless air.

More than tree, but more than symbol. Can
A symbol stand up to its ankles in earth
And fasten consolations on a tired city?

The Minster shouts 'Eternity! Eternity!'
To the dissolving clouds; sits, cold as Latin,
In English speech of leaves that tell the truth

Of the stone's need, its spring and spread and flower.
A rustle of images in a mind that goes
Forward and back to all beginnings.

We must learn to love echoes, correspondences;
Their failure as well as their aptness,
The heraldry of a world we cannot reach.

We must learn the world is not always where
We find ourselves; but we can get to it.
Today it is a garden in a Book of Hours.

Organ pipes are juggling with Bach,
Unreeling him through shivering grisaille. The trees
Move in a green sarabande: *danse lente et grave*.

Between the arguments of Bach and birds
The bride moves in her own time, stepping among
The planes, lifting flowers to an enormous sky.

She stands in fallen leaves and light and ledger lines.

Movement is light and light and leaves and hands
Of lovers under coats. The distant sea
Makes close olfactory puns
From Jeyes Fluid, oilcans, electricity.

A bowlful of gaslight blooms from a tiny gallows,
Cannot fasten on surfaces. It swings,
Sways; a soft boil of yellows.
Moths mill their dirty snow in Saturn rings.

Vermeer light, inside out; a composition
The mind wakes to when not obeying orders;
A small, painterly fiction
That signals truths enlarged beyond its borders.

A train, somewhere, slides slow tons through a pound
And a half of wind. A bell drills like a nerve.
At the platform's chiselled end
Four rails sling moonlight in a perfect curve

That runs all routes through space and time's elisions,
The shape of stories, credences and laughter,
Myth's daily occasions,
The happily we all lived ever after.

The last train creaks in, ticks; doors slam and blow
A muggy yawn of air; shrink intimations
To the tawdry here and now.
But the dull, black rail that hauls trains out of stations

Keeps perfect distance – so many inches – melts
Into a darkness moonlight cannot break
And, packed with quiet volts,
It lopes alongside whichever track we take.

Orpheus

In the end, what was was absence;
The uncouth darkness furred with corpses,
Closer than eyelid of illicit flesh;

Susurrations, a smear on silence;
Between the myrtles, the builders of gaunt dreams,
The artificial living and the small deaths

That go to make up Death. The drowning-place
Where the stalking shades were taught
What bends the lyre breaks the heart.

The punishments of love. At his turning,
Birds flew faster than the images
He had no time to pin them to.

The slow, white shrug of the waterfall
Tipped itself into immobility; light
Stammered, met itself on the way back

From where it had not got to. Fossils formed.
Colour drained. At the bang of the slung
Black wind, each star emptied.

Now, beyond the end of happening, our heads
Sing of despair and the heart is stranded
With its long freight of praise.

Over and over, we translate your missing texts,
Haul black sentences from white paper,
Reflections from the wild, white mirror;

Begin the endless, responsible song
Of being, desiring, of death's deceptions and
The unlimited hospitalities of hell.

until you get it. And when you do, you will, like Jenny Light, find yourself enlightened. Seriously and joyously.

Jack Hawley *The Bhagavad Gita: a Walkthrough for Westerners.*

Exquisitely written and produced, this book from Jenny Light serves as a guiding light to those on the path to self-realization and ascension. As her dearest friend and long-time member of Jenny's devotional meditation group, I know this material well. Her words seep through every pore to the very centre of our being. Her intuitive gifts of leadership, guidance and healing all come into play in these eloquently channelled meditations designed to expand the mind, forge the soul's purpose and reunite us with our own inner Divinity. I know the peace and joy to be gained from regular meditation and this book of guided practices including breath control (pranayama); withdrawal of life-force from the senses (pratyahara); chanting sacred sounds and affirmations; and single-pointed focus and concentration techniques all serve as steps of advancement to the next levels of spiritual attainment. This offering to the Universe is not simply to be read but to be known experientially.

Anita Neilson, author of *Acts of Kindness from your Armchair* (Ayni Books 2017); spiritual poet and kindness blogger at http://anitaneilson.com

Divine Meditations: 26 Spiritual Qualities of The Bhagavad Gita

I recommend this book by Jenny Light to all those who are seeking spiritual Truth. This is the first time that I have seen an author's effort in relating a practical pranayama, a meditation, and an affirmation to each of the 26 Spiritual Qualities of the Bhagavad Gita. It is an interesting and inspiring way to keep us reminded of these spiritual qualities and to practically bring them into our meditation and everyday living. As Jenny says, it is a workbook in the process of getting to know your true Self by clearing out the old mental patterns and establishing new more positive states of being.

Stephen Sturgess, Kriya Yoga meditation teacher (London), disciple of Paramhansa Yogananda, artist and author of *The Yoga Book; The Book of Chakras and Subtle Bodies; Yoga Meditation; The Supreme Art and Science of Raja and Kriya Yoga; Mastering the Mind, Realising the Self.* www.yogananda-kriyayoga.org.uk

Want to make your whole life a meditation? Read this book. There is considerable beauty here, and a great gift in these sacred chapters. Spirituality springs eternal in these leaves. Jenny Light's luminescence beams through every room in the mansion of high spirituality—from the high theory of it through coaching your personal breathing. Everything you need to know shines here, within this book—and within yourself, as you will pleasantly discover. Jam-packed with spot-on, solid spiritual wisdom, shared openly and eagerly by Jenny Light. This is a fine book—so good it should anchor the spiritual wing of your personal library. It's a book to savour, to read again and again

Divine
Meditations

26 Spiritual Qualities of
The Bhagavad Gita

Introduction

Meditation is the conscious process of closing the doors to the bodily senses and going within. Through inward-focused meditation, we embark on the journey to become Self-realised to the light within us is that which inter-connects all things. God-realised inner knowing, learned through meditation, goes beyond words, intellectual understanding or any other mind-based stuff and is realised as an experientially profound truth that is known at the deepest level of being. Self-realisation is God-realisation. The limited tool of the mind cannot encompass anything greater than itself. Self-realisation is to know beyond faith, belief or intellect that 'I am God and blissful Oneness'. There is no sense of other. All simply is. We learn to dive deep in the Ocean of Quiet, awakening to a super-conscious state and therein finding ever-lasting, ever-new bliss in God.

This book is a guide in that process. Until we consciously learn to meditate, we are as if in a walking-sleep state where we have forgotten our Divine heritage and become so attached to the narrative of our own lives that we remain as if asleep. We are as puppets to the reactions of our *samskaras* (karmic impressions) of our past actions. However, we need not remain so. In this book, you will learn how to consciously breathe in a certain way (*pranayama)* to alter your brainwaves into delta waves which will facilitate an easy shift into conscious meditation and then, as your meditation deepens, into the super-conscious state. That is what is meant by a shift in consciousness. The key is being conscious: using the focus of your will, intention and emotion to gaze internally with single-pointed focus. This is another way of saying: Be present. To be absent in the present moment by thinking of the past or concerning about a future, is to remain asleep. You might ask me, how do I know if I am asleep? I will answer you by countering, are you happy all the time, no matter the circumstances around you? Happiness is our natural, God-given state. If you are not happy, it will always be because you are attached to something or someone or some outcome in this physical dream-reality of Earth and that attachment maintains the dream state.

We can dispel this dream-Earth reality to recall that we are a spiritual being temporarily housed in a physical body having a human existence. We may have subconscious memory that while we were in the astral world, we continually created our reality just by thinking, with immediate results. But in the physical world, there is a time delay. Just enough of a time delay to create and maintain an illusion that your thoughts are not powerful and an illusion that our thoughts do not directly create our reality. When the truth is, at any separate moment, our thoughts and desires are creating our very near future as a physical, mental, emotional and spiritual reality. The more illuminated we become, the time delay between thought and manifestation of our desires, becomes shorter until it appears to be happening instantly. You may recognise this fact.

The golden kernel of Universal Truth is found when we focus our soul consciousness in the present moment. Cosmic law decrees that whatever we focus on increases. It becomes manifest until it IS our reality. We create our reality. We have been made in the image of God, as creators. That is what is meant by Jesus when he said: *'These works that I do, shall you also do and greater'* (John 12:14).

So in your Now reality, which goal will you pitch your thought, will and action towards achieving? If meditation is your goal, there is no time better than the present. In each moment, there is a space to slip into meditation. In my seminars, I teach people from all walks of life, to let go of trying and simply be. That might suggest that meditation is like falling into a dream state, such as when we become drowsy before the sleep state. However, this is the polar opposite of the state of meditation. In meditation, we move beyond dream-like fleeting thoughts into sharp single-pointed focus of awareness. The dedicated spiritual person learns to live on a narrow knife-edged path, which becomes increasingly narrow (not to suggest constriction but merely that the balance between right and less right, becomes finer and finer to navigate) as one progresses. However, our sense of intuition and wisdom develops naturally with meditation and we find that knowing what to do, think or say becomes easier as we become more self-monitored on a moment to moment basis, in a very natural way.

You will learn to place your attention away from a thought as it starts to arise. No more to be at the mercy of runaway thoughts and emotions. To abstain from learning to control them via meditation is to remain in ignorance and at the mercy of every knee-jerk emotional reaction to external stimuli or internal storm of emotions. The more we exercise sense withdrawal (*pratyahara*) and introspection in conjunction with meditation, the clearer our choices will be. Material objects which you once desired, quite simply fall away, seemingly without effort. The conscious effort of meditation, over a period of time, creates a bliss of its own, which is alluring for the right reason: it is the vehicle by which you make a divine connection with yourself and God, and to finally realise that you are God and God is all there is. The final result of meditation is to move beyond appearance of duality to *samadhi*, a permanently realised, blissful state of Oneness abiding within all that is.

This book is a workbook in the process of getting to know your true Self, your perfect God-Self by learning to strip away the barriers of illusion that you have erected through many incarnations. The false ego-self is uncovered through identifying with God-like spiritual qualities and becoming that which you focus on. I am not a highly learned person or a Bhagavad Gita pundit. There was a time when I found its language style lofty and elitist. I only know what has been revealed to me through reading and meditating on the Bhagavad Gita and because of that, I revere its scriptural knowledge highly.

In my youth, I was also fiercely averse to guruism in any form but Kundalini-awakening as a child and empathic sensitivity attracted me to yoga and meditation. After meditating for forty years 'in the wilderness', becoming mesmerised by the unceasing wonders of the astral realm, Paramahansa Yogananda's autobiography arrived on my bookshelf. I can't remember how it got there exactly and after several failed attempts to engage with it, it remained unread for ten years. However, there is a right time for everything under the sun and in my fifties, it opened its wisdoms to me. I felt like I had come home! His words unlocked my heart, speaking to me personally from the pages and filled me with a bubbling joy and inner light. I had found my guru and his teachings really opened up wisdom and deepening presence of a personal connection to God within. He leads me out of the physical and inner astral illusions into Cosmic Consciousness within. In taking Paramahansa Yogananda as my beloved guru through the Self-Realization Fellowship, my life is daily in a bliss beyond words or comprehending.

When my guru and guides were preparing me to write this book, they showed me that this book was to be God-consciously 'charged' with higher vibration energy which would catapult the spiritual reader to the next phase on their spiritual unfolding. With this book I hope to awaken many wonderful souls to the truth of their existence here on earth and why they are here.

Learning to *become* the twenty-six spiritual qualities, taken from the Bhagavad Gita, takes us closer to being God-like with each chapter. The discourse in each chapter is not random but has been joyfully revealed to me while in a meditative state to raise the aspirant closer to God just by reading it. Each specific breath practice is designed to traverse the bridge between outer ego-self and inner Self, as a preparation for the deep meditative practice on each particular spiritual quality. These have been realised through me during many meditation teaching groups to lead to a state of bliss in God's all-abiding Being.

It is with deepest love, that I offer this book to you, my reader, to shed Light and Wisdom on your path and aid you on your soul journey home.

Blessings of Love and Light,

Jenny Light

Part 1

Yogic Meditation

Mindfulness has become a very popular solution to living with our busy lifestyles. So many people ask me, what is the difference between mindfulness and meditation? Are they not the same thing? Mindfulness is an act of concentration where we simply become conscious of being in the present moment. It takes will power and intense concentration to train the mind to observe what is arising without a flicker of reaction. It brings detachment and awareness of awareness itself. The mind can be likened to trying to ride a chariot pulled by five strong horses (symbolising the five senses) all pulling in different directions. It takes patience and stamina to rein in the mind to ignore sense stimulation and to focus on one thing only. This is single-pointed focus.

> From whatever cause the restless, unsteady mind wanders away, from that let him restrain it and bring it under the control of the Self alone.
> (Bhagavad Gita 6:26)

Meditation is a deeper, specific focus on realising God. It is the process of withdrawing the senses from the physical body and turning inward, like a tortoise drawing inside its shell. We learn to pull our awareness from the skin, nerves, ears, taste, smell and hearing in order to gaze unwaveringly within, with a focus on knowing God. This takes great resilience and trust to let go of the senses until the body is no longer in our awareness.

> When, like the tortoise which withdraws its limbs on all sides, he withdraws his senses from the sense-objects, then his wisdom becomes steady.
> (Bhagavad Gita 2:58)

Meditation is the means by which we realise our divine spark and God-consciousness in the centre of our being. The word *yoga* means Divine Union. A yogi is he or she who undertakes a scientific practice to God-realisation: a specific approach with empirical results.

Patanjali, who wrote the Yoga Sutras before 400 CE, detailed an eightfold path as a self-disciplined moral and ethical code of conduct to lead the yogi inward to see through the cosmic illusion (*maya*) of the external world to reveal who we are: what is real (all pervading bliss in God-consciousness) and what is unreal (ego). We learn to identify what is true and to be non-reactive to anything false, in an increasingly subtle revelation of God, hiding within us in plain sight.

Patanjali's eight-step path to enlightenment is:

1. *Yamas* – Five ethical standards which relate to our behaviour and how we conduct ourselves in life. Through these we learn to live with integrity in all our dealings with others, and towards ourselves. The five *yamas* are: *ahimsa* (nonviolence), *satya* (truthfulness), *asteya* (nonstealing), *brahmacharya* (continence) and *aparigraha* (noncovetousness).

2. *Niyamas* – Five standards of self-discipline and spiritual observances. The five *niyamas* are: *saucha* (cleanliness), *samtosa* (contentment), *tapas* (heat; spiritual austerities), *svadhyaya* (right study of the sacred scriptures), *isvara pranidhana* (surrender to God). (The *yamas* and *niyamas* will be explored and developed later within the spiritual qualities in Part 3.)

3. *Asanas* – The postures practised in yoga which honour and care for the physical body as a temple that the soul is housed in during an incarnation. Through the practice of physical *asanas*, we develop the habit of discipline, physical stamina and the ability to concentrate. However,

it should be pointed out that the ultimate goal of *asana* is God-consciousness, therefore to practise yoga postures mindlessly, is not to be practising yoga. Neither is asana true yoga (divine union) if it is executed with ego fixated on our outer appearance to others.

Some *asana* or exercise prior to meditation is beneficial in order to quieten the mind, so that it will allow you to sit. The sole reason for *asana* is to prepare the physical body to sit for longer and longer periods of time in absolute immobility (even stilling the breath eventually). Indeed, Patanjali referred to the ultimate asana: the seated posture for meditation. Complete motionlessness in the seated position for an hour or more indicates a mastery of the mind and body. During meditation, any tiny movement of the physical body gives feedback to the mind (*manus*) via the senses of where the body is in space, which is counter-productive to moving beyond false identification with ego (*ahamkara*). Holding *asana* postures helps to build that focus and stamina.

As a natural part of spiritual development, the ratio of importance of asana to meditation shifts from 90% *asana*: 10% meditation to 90% meditation: 10% *asana*. This development is not necessarily related to the physical age of the person but is concerned with one's spiritual commitment to becoming God-conscious.

4. ***Pranayama*** – This is often mistakenly translated as 'breath control'. *Prana* meaning 'life' strictly means 'life control'. This fourth stage is a focus on breath techniques intended to change the brainwave patterns from the normal beta waves into the theta and delta waves of deep meditation.

Beta (14-30 waves per second (Hz)) is the normal waking state when attention is directed to the outer world. When the brain is in Alpha waves (9-13Hz) you feel truly relaxed. This is where meditation starts and you begin to access the creativity of the astral world. However, alpha is also the state of sleep which is why some people need to guard against falling asleep as the brain makes the transition from beta to alpha. Theta (4-8 Hz) is deep sleep state or super-consciously in meditation. Theta brings forward flashes of dreamlike imagery, intuition and a sensation of floating in a waking dream. When you learn to traverse this inner astral landscape without being distracted, you move into delta waves (1-3 Hz), which is the slowest of brainwave activity found during deep, dreamless sleep and present in very experienced meditators.

In this book, you will learn how to consciously change the oscillations of the brainwaves as you move into deeper meditation by using the breath as a tool to slide consciously into deeper and deeper experience of controlling mental brainwave fluctuation. Thus, by focusing on the breath, we learn to slow the brain, the mind and the body processes into a state conducive to meditation.

Focus on the breath will increase *prana*, or life force, in the body and reverse the decay of the physical body. Most importantly, we learn that the breath contains a bridge between consciousness of the physical body and the inner reality of the astral and causal universes. Or more specifically, the breath is the entrance to the bridge, between small 'I' or ego consciousness and God. The bridge itself is *sandhi*, the junction of awareness, stillness and cosmic presence.

5. ***Pratyahara*** – The fifth limb means withdrawal or sensory transcendence. It is the conscious effort to draw our awareness away from the illusion of the external world. The five senses operate to give us continuous feedback to the ego. We are housed in an illusory body in an illusory external world. In order to realise the truth, we learn to divert our attention away from outside stimuli and

towards inward focus.

6. *Dharana* – The practice of concentration, which precedes meditation, where we learn how to hone the thinking process by concentrating on a single mental object. This is single-pointed focus. It takes great attention to keep the mind focused on one thing to the exclusion of all thoughts which will certainly plague the beginner. This is also called mindfulness.

   Dharana is practised during all of the eight limbs of yoga: if there is not concentration in the present moment, then there is no yoga.

7. *Dhyana* – Meditation or contemplation is the uninterrupted flow of concentration on God. Although concentration (*dharana*) and meditation (*dhyana*) may appear to be one and the same, *dharana* practises one-pointed attention, in *dhyana* we increasingly move into a state of greater awareness of God as bliss. At this stage, the ego-mind has been quieted, and in the stillness it produces few or no thoughts at all. It takes great persistence, strength and stamina to reach this state of peace and inner joy. This is the penultimate experience before attaining yoga (divine union) for at this stage the yogi still experiences duality of the soul and God as separate. Attention has been withdrawn from external physical senses and is wholly fixed within.

   Patanjali referred to meditation as '*chitti vriitti nirodhah*' which means, Restraint from Mental Fluctuations. You may reflect on the stability of your mental state in a normal day. When do you feel clear, aware and stable? Is it a particular time of day? Or do you feel stable only when life is going your way? Are there any particular triggers to emotional mood-swings or mental fluctuations? What if mental fluctuations were not real? What if you could nullify mental fluctuation through a conscious act of will?

By developing great inner control and focus through long periods of meditation, you will learn to de-invest in inner mental fluctuation and just learn to Be who you truly are. These treasures are all in store for you when you dive deeply for prolonged periods in meditation.

8. *Samadhi* – Being totally immersed, a state of ever-new bliss or God-realisation. At this stage, the yogi realises as experiential truth, a profound interconnectedness with all living things. You realise that you *are* God. There is only unity: there is no experience of 'other'. This divine union is experienced as bliss: a deep 'peace that surpasses all understanding' and being at one with the whole of creation.

There are two distinct phases of *samadhi*. With reference to advanced stages of realisation, in *savrikalpa* (with difference)*samadhi*, there still remains some duality between the knower and the known, such as in the phrase: 'God and I are One.' But in *nirvikalpa* (without difference) *samadhi*, all distinctions are resolved into One Spirit. God is the only reality. This latter stage of *samadhi* is the highest yoga or union manifested by fully liberated masters or those on the threshold of soul freedom.

Patanjali goes on to divide the earlier stage of *savrikalpa samadhi* into four levels: Firstly, *savritarka* (with doubt) where intuitive experience is mixed with a doubt-ridden mind. Secondly, *savichara* (with reasoning) where intuitive experience is mixed with discrimination guided intellect. Thirdly, *sananda* (with joy) as interiorised intuitive experience as joy-permeated feeling. Lastly, *sasmita* (with 'I'-ness) as intuitive experience mixed with a pure sense of Being. There can be some movement between these levels with experience of duality until there is permanent union in *nirvikalpa samadhi* as God.

Enlightenment can neither be bought nor possessed. This ultimate stage of yoga can only be experienced.

Ever-lasting, ever-new joy and divine bliss is the result of the continual devotion of the aspirant on God. God is Love and love is the language of God's creation. While there is still an illusion of separateness of I and God, it is love which gets the attention of God. God can bestow divine grace (*anugraha*) which can come to anyone at any time, regardless of one's efforts. However, as in all things worthwhile, practice makes perfect or rather, through practice we can realise inner perfection and become more receptive to grace through the stilling of the mind.

The length of the task to achieve the results of peace and self-realisation may seem daunting. However, I would like to reiterate that the Universe around you will support you in finding Oneness. God wants us to know that Oneness and Bliss, which we once consciously knew, has placed an irresistible longing in our hearts to be in that state of being once more. No matter how many eons and incarnations you have been pleasure-engrossed in, ego-driven desires and illusion or what karma you may have garnered, that inner longing is calling us home. We find, when we start to meditate deeply, that we were never away from God's Love and blissfulness, we just chose to let the ego, with its earthly desires and earth-bound beliefs, have sway over our higher conscious self.

There is nothing that you have done which exempts you from God's Love, for does not a father love his child, even if that child errs and falters at times? God has Unconditional Love for you that does not judge or falter but waits patiently for you to turn to Him, at last heeding the call of your soul's longing to turn away from the glittering baubles of materialism, by going within.

Fixing thy mind on Me, thou shalt by My Grace overcome all obstacles.
(Bhagavad Gita 18:62)

15

And at some point, early on, most people find that they get quick positive feedback as a reward for meditating. Call it beginner's luck. I personally think that God wants us to be drawn back to Him and every day he calls to us to sit and face inward to reconnect with our inner God-spark. It is part of God's plan that there is easy payback or dividends after one or two sessions of sitting in the quiet. Namely: increased peacefulness, less agitation, a sense of homecoming, bubbles of joy, spontaneous laughter etc. This is to help us to establish that routine and a discipline to maintain meditation.

In this book we will be using a tried and tested yogic approach to God-realisation. This includes specific breath practices (*pranayama*) to calm the mind and senses and to channel *prana* (life force) within the energy channels of the psychic anatomy away from physical, emotional or mental distractions. As a starting place for meditation, the breath practice sets the scene. You will learn that within 12 or more easy breaths, you will have loosened ties to physical awareness and ego-led thoughts, to create a platform with which to dive deep into meditation. '*Yama*' means 'control' or 'restriction' and 'prana' means 'breath' or 'life force'. *Pranayama* means literally: 'control of life-force'. That is to say, we learn to move beyond an unconscious process of breathing in order to supply the physical body with air, to consciously breathing and moving the life force in the subtle body. It is only by being consciously present and aware of the breath that the truth of the Reality of Life and who you really are is revealed. Ask yourself, how many breaths in the day am I conscious that the body is breathing? When we master our breath, we are in control of our bodies and minds. Early on in your meditation practice, you will experience a noticeable indication that your attempt to sit in silence and go within is creating results. These, I am sure, are designed by God to show us clearly that the path we are embarking on is the right path. A trail of breadcrumbs if you like. Common experiences are a deeper sense of peace than hitherto, a sensation of heat in the hands, an awareness of tingling in the body, a perception of blue or gold light or hearing high pitched sound. Each person's experience is as unique as their fingerprint. While one person may see dancing blue light from their first attempt to meditate,just trust that something is happening, even in the absence of any feedback to the contrary. Be aware that it is the ego which needs constant verification of where it is in space or external events all the time in order to exist within the human experience. An expectation of having a certain 'experience' creates a mental wave of agitation which is a hindrance to making deep conscious contact with your inner self or God. If you can sit still without moving physically (apart from the breath) the ego will eventually be quiet. It is my experience that if you persevere in your practice, you will become aware of a deepening peace and lasting stillness.

There will be times, dear hearts, when you feel that you are not making any progress with your meditation practice. It may often feel that nothing is happening at all. Be prepared for times when you apply Faith and keep going in trust, in the absence of any evidence to the contrary. Just know that you are on the right trail. Treat each moment with a fresh anticipation that a greater depth will arise as you are blessed with another breadcrumb. There is no guilt on this path. Even if you should fail from the ideal, just pick yourself up, dust yourself off and try again.

Let 'keep on, keeping on' be your motto.

I ask my students to visualise that with every commitment they make to meditation, they are metaphorically placing a stone on a cairn. With each sitting, each mindful thought, another stone is placed on the growing pile until, before long, they have built a substantial mound, each stone, a testament to their persistent effort to meditate: small pebbles for short periods; larger stones when your meditation practice becomes deeper, longer and you experience less mental fluctuations in daily life; huge boulders as the intensity of focus increases and you become absorbed in inner bliss. Before very long, you will have a monumental cairn as a testament to your persistent effort. The good news is that it is never too late to begin and any spiritual progress that you make, unlike material goods, will be carried in your soul at the transition of body-death and directly relate to how favourable your circumstances are in your next incarnation.

This visualisation helps remind us that we are fulfilling a spiritual commitment to knowing God. In the times when there is no evidence of effect, we can remind ourselves that in doggedly continuing, we are creating a substantive change in ourselves. And it is at these times of faith and persistence in the face of lack of evidence, that we are making the most progress.

In fact, all singing, all dancing visual displays, sounds or sensations are just the icing on the cake. They are not the cake itself. I warn you to be vigilant against becoming mesmerised by any energy displays. Entrancement here would merely replace one *maya* (illusion) of the physical realm for another illusion of the astral realm. The meditation student should ignore them as a distraction on the inward path and keep seeking a deeper and deeper connection with God within. Having broken through into the inner realm, without guidance on which path to follow, to arrive at Oneness, one can lose one's way, rather like Alice in Wonderland.

Establishing a daily practice

Try to be disciplined and attempt to meditate every day. You will need to establish a daily routine to meditate to feel the benefits. Don't be disheartened if you don't seem to touch that quiet within you – rest assured that the very act of trying helps to establish the ground work, even on those days when it seems impossible. The act of making the effort to sit has gone one step on the way to linking with the process. In fact, not every period that you sit will feel successful, but as you go on you will realise that the days when nothing seems to be happening are the times when the most growth is being found.

It is a good idea to practise at the same time every day. It becomes a habit, like always brushing your teeth at a certain time, which the mind becomes comfortable with. It is advantageous to meditate at times when the earth and the world around you are quiet; whether we are consciously aware of the busy thought-waves of others or not, we sub-consciously experience any mental 'busy-ness' in our vicinity. Not only is there mental unrest within but there can be more external busy-ness at certain times of the day. Experienced meditators develop a sensitivity to perceive the mental thought-waves and emotions of others. That is one reason why early morning and late evening meditations are so beneficial. The other reason is of deeper significance: Choosing to meditate before interacting with the events of your day creates a platform or basis for the whole day. Before taking on the role and mantle of the day, taking time to observe inner quiet and divine connection will have noticeable repercussions: externally, traffic lights change to green, life flows seamlessly, people respond more favourably; internally, thoughts are clearer, emotions calmer and you will feel more spontaneously disposed to compassion and generosity. Further, deviations from the inner calm are more noticeable as if they are happening to someone else. This distancing from the drama of your life and from any internal reactions, develops so that you can experience the quiet Self as something other than events, circumstances, mind or emotions.

Choosing to meditate at the end of the day before sleep makes a statement of intent to the subconscious, leading you to continue divine union while in the sleep state. You will learn that there is no 'off' day. We are continually working to realise our essential nature, even in the sleeping state.

Think of a time in your schedule when are able to commit twenty or thirty minutes to God. On the days when you miss your usual meditation time, try to touch base with your practice later in the day, even for a shorter period. Eventually, you may wish to establish a morning meditation practice and an evening one, one of these being your longer main practice. This establishes an umbrella of attention over your day, from the firmament of the morning meditation platform, to a regrouping of intent and self-analysis at the evening practice. Through inner reflection, you may reveal decreasing emotional reaction to events and greater inner peace, during each successive day.

Set up a personal meditation space

If you set up an environment for the practice of meditation, when you enter that space, your mind with recognise that you are there for meditation and the ego will learn to not hinder the progress. You should have a space in your room where you can sit comfortably. Have a small table where you can light a candle at, or slightly below, eye level. Place a few items on the table which inspire you, such as crystals, angel cards, a symbolic statue, photograph, incense or flowers.

Have a specific cushion or blanket that you use, which is a signal to the mind that you are about to meditate and is helpful in the establishment of a good habit. This blanket and cushion will become charged with magnetic spiritual energy from practising meditation so that this is also conducive to meditation by sending a message to the body, mind and spirit to move into the delta brainwaves of meditation.

Having silence to listen to the inner sound is important. Many students find a guided meditation helpful and while this may have some benefit for a beginner to meditation, there is no shortcut. In becoming Self-realised, we must have silence to listen deeply within. Try to make your environment as quiet as possible. That is not to say that external noise beyond your control is bad, only try to accept whatever noise arises around you without allowing distraction away from the inner goal.

No one can do this work for you. An illumined master can

point you in the right direction and can even give realisation to advanced students through *shaktipata* but it is you who must make the sincere effort required to pass to the next level.

Preparation for meditation

Try not to eat a heavy meal beforehand as it can tend to make you sleepy. The journey of meditation is to retain focus. The mind will be more conducive to sitting after a short period of yoga to settle the body.

Choose a sitting position where you can sit comfortably without moving for a long period. It is not important whether you sit comfortably on the floor, in a chair or in a sitting stool, as long as the spine is straight. This is highly important as the main energy channel in the spine (*sushumna*) must be straight in order to allow the life force (*prana*) to flow. As much as 50% of *prana* flow can be limited when the spine is not erect.

Once you have settled in your preferred seated position, tip your spine forward a few centimetres. Become aware of the base of the spine. Maintaining consciousness of the vertebrae, slowly bring your spine erect, as if aligning each vertebra, one on top of the next. Feel the connected flow of energy or *prana* between the base of the spine and the neck and head.

Check your posture and make adjustment where necessary so that you are comfortable. You need to feel completely relaxed but at the same time completely alert.

Affirmation and Prayer

Each chapter in this book has a particular affirmation or prayer which has been selected to help you clear out old patterns and establish new, more positive states of being. Affirmation is one tool towards cultivating, nurturing and manifesting God-like qualities until they can naturally arise with profound presence and effect in the realised being.

The goal of yoga is to transcend the seeming separateness

and the pairs of opposites, not necessarily just to improve the personality and the external life as such. This might seem at times to be a building up (of knowledge, techniques, qualities and experiences) but then it becomes much more of a stripping down. It becomes a paring back of ego-induced non-reality to reveal absolute reality, veil by veil. Using affirmation can be helpful in establishing new traits and cultivating a more fertile foundation for this yogic process.

Affirmation is a prayer-demand to God to imbue you with the specific spiritual quality becoming established in each chapter. Use an affirmation before your meditation practice. For maximum effectiveness, also use affirmations immediately after waking in the morning or just before falling asleep at night. Placing reminders as post-it notes on the bathroom mirror or as a screen-saver can help you to recall and repeat an affirmation at additional times during the day.

Sit with spine erect. Close your eyes and gently focus your gaze and concentrate at the point between the eyebrows, the back of the head or the heart. Inhale and exhale deeply three times. Relax the body and keep it motionless.

Affirmation can be spoken aloud (with feeling or will), whispered softly and more slowly, or mentally only, without moving the tongue or the lips, until you feel that you have attained deep, unbroken concentration. This is not unconsciousness, but a profound continuity of uninterrupted thought. If you continue with your mental affirmation, and go still deeper, you will feel a sense of increasing joy and peace.

In order to be most powerful and effective, hold an intensity of attention in your affirmation. Repeat with devotion, will, and faith between 5 and 108 times. Affirmation is then like a highly explosive vibration bomb, which shatters rocks of difficulties and creates the change desired. So that change is lasting, aim to reach both the subconscious and super-conscious states.

Spoken words are sounds caused by the vibrations of

thoughts. Thoughts are vibrations sent forth by the ego or by the soul. Every word you utter can be potent with soul vibration but your words are lifeless if you fail to fill them with the spiritual force of intensity of attention.

Grounding

As a pre-cursor to any meditation session, it is important to learn to ground your energies into the Earth. This helps us to:

1. Discharge pent up negative electrical charge or emotions
2. Link with our present incarnation by linking with the earth herself
3. Balance our physical, mental and emotional energies

If we take the analogy of a tree, the deeper the roots, the taller the tree can grow. When we ground our energy into the earth, we are making a conscious statement that we are willing to trust in the process of this incarnation to bring us to Self-realisation.

Tree Meditation

Consciously breathe in and breathe out through your tail bone, down through your roots into the earth. Connect with the golden light at the heart of the planet. See, feel or visualise it as a pool of golden light. Allow yourself to let go and become immersed in this cleansing light, much like swimming in water. Experience being cleansed and absolved of any issues or worries that you have been carrying.

Flow upward with gratitude through your roots, into the heart. Imagine golden light circulating around your heart. Flow upwards through the crown of the head into a golden sun above your head. Allow yourself to be bathed in this fine quality golden light. Imagine gold light is showering your entire body inside and out, as if you are hollow.

Breathe golden light down into the heart. The heart is

connecting golden light from above and from the earth. Imagine golden light flowing down the back, back of the legs, under the feet, up the front of the body, down over the head, back of the neck and shoulders. Be aware of being within a golden bubble of light.

In your imagination, open into a wood, in your inner world. Trees of all kinds stand in stately communion with one another. One tree takes your attention. Allow yourself to connect with the tree. Listen to it. Feel how it feels. Imagine that you become the tree. Experience your roots growing into the earth as the tree's roots. Feel the deep communion which you have with the earth beneath, as if you and the earth were one being.

Your roots give you a firm, connected base. Know that you are the earth beneath.

Breathe earth energy up, into the heart. From the heart, breathe out that earth energy into branches, extending in all directions. Invite and welcome small birds to play in your branches. Notice how infectious their joy is.

Breathe your consciousness into the heart of a bird. Open your wings and fly free. Experience the air as a golden current of light, buoyant and carefree. Feel joy in the freedom to soar and express yourself as unfettered.

Allow the image to fade and become One with your heart. In that boundless space behind the physical heart, let go of everything by handing it over to the Divine.

Affirm quietly and with confidence: *'I am Love'*.

Mentally repeat several times. Bask in this affirmation. Allow the affirmation to be ever-new and in the moment by really focusing on the words and the message behind the words. Seek with an enquiring mind to find new meaning in the mantra. Notice and release any reactions which percolate up from the depth of you. Practise non-attention.

Part 2

Taking it deeper through the Bhagavad Gita's twenty-six soul qualities that make us God-like

Sri Krishna's message in the Bhagavad Gita is the perfect answer for the modern age and any age: Yoga of dutiful action, of nonattachment, and of meditation for God-realisation. To work without the inner peace of God is Hades and to work with His joy ever bubbling through the soul is to carry a portable paradise within wherever one goes.

(Paramahansa Yogananda, *The Yoga of the Bhagavad Gita*)

Bhagavad Gita means *'Song of the Spirit'*. Although it was reputed to have been written five thousand years ago, is still a practical how-to-live message for the modern person. With a choice between remaining to live as an ignorant, selfish person in the world or the spiritual life of an ascetic living in seclusion from the world, the Gita teaches a middle way. The Gita charts how to be in the world and how to keep the mind trained on realising God-consciousness while one acts in the world. Self-realisation is to realise that it is not 'I' who performs any actions but God, since God is behind this patterned curtain of physical reality.

Be in the world but not of the world

As the journey of life starts with the longest and most difficult first step, by incarnating again here on Earth, we find ourselves, like Arjuna, the main character, who represents the awakening soul, facing our inner self on the battlefield of life. The challenges which we meet here are intended to pull us up short in order to enquire into the nature of reality and how we fit within that illusive elastic backdrop. Who am I? And why am I here?

From the very first moment of conception to the release of the last breath on Earth, in each incarnation we have to fight many moral, psychological and spiritual battles. Life's lesson is to choose to act wisely when faced with opposing forces of good or evil (forces that liberate or forces that contract/bind) behind every encounter in this life.

The beginning of the historic saga depicted in the Gita, part of the larger Mahabharata, opens with Arjuna on a battlefield questioning his ability to continue with his role and the whole meaning of life. Bhagavan (Lord) Krishna, as his charioteer, guides him through the time-honoured question and answer format of disciple and guru. So in a very real sense, Krishna reminds us that the wake-up call to the Divine Reality of macrocosmic creation within a microcosmic spiritual epiphany within the drama unfolding in our own incarnation, can happen at any time to each of us. The Gita cleverly weaves great spiritual wisdoms and pathways to God-realisation as liberation from continued soul-bondage from the cycle of birth and rebirth. To be born in a physical body at all is a sign that you have much to learn, although an enlightened master may choose to incarnate to lead brother/sister souls out of karmic bondage.

Parmanahansa Yogananda said that his master, Sri Yukteswar, taught him the virtues of direct realisation of knowledge from the Gita, or any spiritual text, through deep intense meditation and spiritual enquiry with the illumined master who wrote it. As such, the crystallisation of the knowledge contained in each stanza is downloaded as firsthand experience, not mere intellectual knowledge. This knowledge is beheld as a living truth, profoundly real, beyond words, like a chalice of golden light perceived in the heart, brimming over with an intense bliss. You will know what I mean if you have ever had an epiphany: earth shattering lightning to your core which shakes the very foundations of all that you believed was reality. St Teresa of Avila refers to these moments as favours from God. The good news is that these are not exclusive to Divine Masters. Divine realisation is available to every soul who deeply, sincerely seeks to know and love God.

On the battlefield, Arjuna has a wake-up call: he sees his family and loved ones lining the opposing side and states to Krishna that he cannot fight. He is full of despondency and in a bad place emotionally and mentally. The metaphor here is of the battlefield of the drama of our own lives and in a very real sense, the loves ones in our lives are the ones who challenge us the most. But on a deeper level, this is an internal battle which is alluded to: the battle to gain Divine supremacy over little ego's will which, inherently attached to sense allure and gratification, keeps the soul bound to body consciousness as a false reality. While Krishna guides Arjuna in making wise choices within his God-appointed role in the external drama, He is, on a spiritual level, leading his devotee to deeper and deeper awareness of God, the unseen dramatist behind the whole of created physical cosmos, astral cosmos and causal cosmos. The journey which Arjuna undertook by incarnating is the same for all of us within our own soul journey through multitudinous lifetimes. We seek to find soul freedom from being bound to the wheel of birth and rebirth (karma) as a barrier to total Divine Union. Karmic debt can be both pre-natal karma incurred over many incarnations and post-natal karma through ego-driven choices in this incarnation.

Karmic debts, then, influence the next incarnation within a family and those key souls whom you are predestined to meet at appointed junctures within life to learn to redress all debts through acceptance of the past, forgiveness and by loving them unconditionally. Obviously, it takes many, many lifetimes to release karma and in the process of incarnating we run the risk of incurring more karma. The Bhagavad Gita offers us another way. The Christ Consciousness through Lord Krishna guides us to renounce all desires springing from the ego and its attachments to the bodily senses which cause us to feel separate from God as the Cosmic Dreamer. The Gita teaches us how to reach *samadhi*, blissful yoga meditation, by dissolving the compelling forces of this delusive earthly reality as a duality between Self and Spirit. In the final stage of *samadhi*, the dream delusion terminates as we awaken in Oneness with pure cosmic consciousness with God as ever-lasting, ever-conscious ecstatic bliss. Jesus promised that this reality was true for any sincere seeker.

> *So I say to you: Ask and it will be given to you; seek and you will find.*
> (Luke 11:9)

'Christ' and 'Krishna' are not titles but a high level of consciousness conferred on divine souls who have attained Universal Christ or Krishna Consciousness as oneness with God while in incarnation. Jesus Christ and Bhagavan Krishna, are perfected beings who chose to come back to Earth to draw a virtue back to the fore to lift the spirits of the general populace and to illumine the pathway to full God-realisation for as many souls as will listen.

And so, we return to the chronicled historical backdrop laden with symbolic spiritual signposts within the Gita. Krishna was born to his imprisoned mother and secretly carried through mysteriously unlocked doors to his foster home with two cowherds. His childhood is peppered with tales of his incredible powers and displays of his wisdom. Once, when Krishna was gorging himself on freshly made cheese, on prising open his mouth to avoid his choking, his foster mother saw within his open mouth the whole of creation in the cosmos, including her own form. Krishna is often depicted as blue, the colour of Christ Consciousness, which can be seen through the brow chakra of those in deep meditation. While hardly more than a boy, Krishna's worldly role began by seeking to mediate between the two warring factions of the same family: the Pandavas and the Kauravas. Their fathers were brothers but the Pandavas's father, King Pandu, died leaving his five children under the care of their grandfather, Bhishma who was forced to rule until Pandu's eldest son, Yudhistthira, was old enough to rule. Pandu's younger brother, Dhritarashtra, being born blind (symbolising the blind will of the ego), could not rule the kingdom. So Pandu's sons and Dhritarashtra's one hundred sons all grew up together. Duryodhana, the eldest of Dhritarashtra's sons became intensely jealous and angry as Yudhishthira became old enough to be crowned king. After several unsuccessful attempts to kill Pandu's sons, he finally succeeded in using trickery to exile them from the kingdom for thirteen years. When they returned from exile, Duryodhana refused to give them back the kingdom as he had promised.

So, the peace-loving Yudhishana was forced to fight for right. His courageous brother Arjuna and the devious Duryodhana went to appeal to Krishna, said to be the embodiment of Divine and the Supreme Lord, for a solution. The all-wise Krishna gave them a choice between having Himself as their personal charioteer, but would not take part in the battle, or to have all His armies. Immediately, the wise Arjuna chooses Krishna as his guide and guru. Duryodhana, delighted to receive all the armies, is convinced that he will win. The name of each character in this saga has mystical meaning passed down from generation to generation of yoga masters.

Symbolically, this is the scene as the Gita dialogue commences: man's soul consciousness (realisation of Eternal Blissful Oneness) has descended through various graduations to human body-consciousness. The senses (the five horses) linked to the blind mind (the blind King Dhritarashtra) as well as the power of pure discrimination rule in the bodily kingdom (chariot). There is constant conflict between the forces of the materialistic senses, focused on pure external pleasure, and pure discrimination that tries to return the soul's consciousness to its natural state of God-realisation. The internal battle rests within the mind.

The Bhagavad Gita is written in eighteen chapters as a

dialogue between the two main characters, Arjuna and Krishna. Arjuna represents our awakening soul consciousness who having reached the 'enough' point in the human condition of perpetual cycle of life, death and rebirth, wants to find that eternal harmony and union with God, which is yoga. Arjuna, through Krishna's guidance, realises the many devious ways that the ego binds us karmically to the human condition. Krishna, as the realised Christ Consciousness, represents the divine right and heritage of every sincere soul seeking enlightenment. When we have turned away from the bedazzlement of this material world and seek within instead, like Arjuna, the right teacher appears for us.

The Bhagavad Gita lays out in great detail an explicit path to divine consciousness. Meditation is not shutting one's eyes and coming into a relaxed sleepiness: this is merely relaxation. Nor is meditation solely single-pointed focus: this is concentration of the mind, which is an aspect of meditation, but not meditation itself. The Bhagavad Gita details for us how to know God-union through inner renunciation of our actions and the results of those actions to God and through meditation on God.

Meditation has been the mainstay of my life and the calm in the eye of the storm since the age of fourteen. Meditation is my first port of call when I have to make a difficult choice or when my world has seemingly turned upside down. It is my stable foundation. Even when the waves threaten to swamp me, I turn within, focus on breathing and resume calm inner focus. Years of practice has prepared me for the teachings of the great masters, Jesus Christ and Guru Paramahansa Yoganananda and for the great Indian scripture, the Bhagavad Gita. I am humbled to be in the presence of noble, pure souls and to be entrusted with the task of guiding other souls away from the allure of materialism and physical illusion to the inward-turning God-realisation through meditation.

Make no mistake. Meditation is the single most important thing you could do with this life. No other pursuit will have soul-fulfilling impact from the moment you start and be carried beyond the veil at physical death. There are no pockets in a shroud: the glitter and amassing of material gain vanishes as the astral body flies free of the physical cage. In that instant, we glimpse the divine heritage which we failed to grasp while in the physical, which was to be found within. We realise that outward attention on the cosmic delusion held us transfixed. It's a Truman moment of waking up and realising that all other characters are just playing a part in the drama of your life to enable you to awaken to your divine role. Shakespeare perceived the cosmic reality when he said:

All the world's a stage,
And all the men and women merely players;
They have their exits and their entrances,
And one man in his time plays many parts.
(Shakespeare, *'As You Like It'*)

This book is a step-by-step guide into deep communion with God by stripping away all the illusion of what-you-are-not to reveal the only reality: you are soul perfection in Oneness with creation and all that is. The Bhagavad Gita clearly outlines twenty-six spiritual qualities for living here on Earth to help us to be God-like. God so dearly calls us to return within the fold that in every era He has sent great masters to alleviate karmic struggle and illumine the path home. Scriptural writings as well as oral tradition have been the means of holding the high vibration message of great masters from era to era.

The intent of the Bhagavad Gita is to lift man's efforts beyond 'evil' tendencies which lead to ignorance and delusion, and repel the consciousness from God to align with righteousness (*dharma*), with the ultimate aim of Self-realisation: the realisation of one's true Self, the soul, as made in the image of God, one with the ever-lasting, ever-conscious, ever-new bliss of Spirit. As long as we continue blaming others for any ill feeling or remain locked into seeking external stimuli, we remain blind to our true Self-consciousness. How then shall we act, think and speak in this world to bring us nearer to God consciousness?

The Bhagavad Gita charts twenty-six soul qualities for the soul to emulate a state of being be good or God-like. God-like is that which expresses truth, virtue and attracts our consciousness to God. It is a process of becoming conscious of sloughing off the delusive non-reality of *maya* to reveal God as the only true reality.

In order to realise each soul quality, the soul must align his or herself with each quality in turn through:

- prayer as a personal appeal to God to reveal the true reality
- personal introspection de-investing with attachments to people, place or actions, through emulation and 'trying on' the quality , just be it
- meditation by just *being* a specific quality

How do we learn anything in life? By trying it on for size and learning how it feels to approach life and everything in it in a different way. Using the analogy of being in love is to see the world through rose-coloured spectacles, we can understand that it is not that external circumstance or person which 'makes' us feel negative or positive, it is our own state of being; that, we have choice over. We can choose to change our mode of being. When you meditate on each spiritual quality, try not to just entertain a mental concept of it, but imagine you were in a sphere immersed in that quality, that it fills you inside and that you look out upon the external world through this highly magnetically charged space.

Take, for example, the quality *ahimsa* (non-harming of self and others) as a daily practice.

1. Use prayer to raise your soul consciousness or vibratory rate by aligning with the masters who are God-realised or with God directly
2. Read and reflect on the discourse around the meaning and acquisition of realising *ahimsa*
3. Meditate using the steps in the guided meditation on *ahimsa*. Imagine you are bathed in the quality inside and out
4. Reflect on God as the quality of *ahimsa* and hold no intention to cause pain or harm. God is the shelter from all harm. Any harm that arises is from our deluded identification with the illusive world of duality
5. Use the affirmation several times in the day to reconnect your consciousness to the divine quality of *ahimsa*
6. On a daily basis, revisit *ahimsa* until you start to find that quality arising from within in your daily life beyond your meditation practice (2-4 weeks as a guideline)

In chapter sixteen of the Bhagavad Gita, we find the list of the twenty-six God-like qualities to emulate in our journey of stripping away that-which-we-are-not (the dualist illusion of creation) and to reveal the cosmic reality of ever-present bliss in God within.

The 26 Spiritual Qualities:
Bhagavad Gita 16:1-3

1 श्रीपरमात्मने नमः
अथ षोडशोऽध्यायः
श्रीभगवानुवाच
अभयं सत्त्वसंशुद्धिर्ज्ञानयोगव्यवस्थितिः ।
दानं दमश्च यज्ञश्च स्वाध्यायस्तप आर्जवम् ॥१६- १॥
अभयम् fearlessness, सत्त्वसंशुद्धिः purity of heart, ज्ञानयोगव्यवस्थितिः steadfastness in knowledge and Yoga,

35

दानम् almsgiving, दमः control of the senses, च and यज्ञः sacrifice, च and स्वाध्यायः study of Sastras, तपः austerity, आर्जवम् straightforwardness.

śrī-bhagavān uvāca

abhayaṁ sattva-saṁśuddhir jñāna-yoga-vyavasthitiḥ

dānaṁ damaś ca yajñaś ca svādhyāyas tapa ārjavam

2 अहिंसा सत्यमक्रोधस्त्यागः शान्तिरपैशुनम् ।
   दया भूतेष्वलोलुप्त्वं मार्दवं ह्रीरचापलम् ॥१६- २॥

अहिंसा harmlessness, सत्यम् truth, अक्रोधः absence of anger, त्यागः renunciation, शान्तिः peacefulness, अपैशुनम् absence of crookedness, दया compassion भूतेषु in beings, अलोलुप्त्वम् noncovetousness, मार्दवम् gentleness, ह्रीः modesty, अचापलम् absence of fickleness.

ahiṁsā satyam akrodhas tyāgaḥ śāntir apaiśunaṁ

dayā bhūteṣv aloluptvaṁ mārdavaṁ hrīr acāpalam

3 तेजः क्षमा धृतिः शौचमद्रोहो नातिमानिता ।
   भवन्ति संपदं दैवीमभिजातस्य भारत ॥१६- ३॥

तेजः vigour, क्षमा forgiveness, धृतिः fortitude, शौचम् purity, अद्रोहः absence of hatred, नातिमानिता absence of conceit, भवन्ति belong, सम्पदम् state, दैवीम् divine, अभिजातस्य to the one born for, भारत O descendant of Bharata (Arjuna).

tejaḥ kṣamā dhṛtiḥ śaucam adroho nāti-mānitā

bhavanti saṁpadaṁ daivīm abhijātasya bhārata

The Blessed Lord said:

1. *Fearlessness, purity of heart, steadfastness in Yoga and knowledge, alms-giving control of the senses, sacrifice, study of scriptures, austerity and straightforwardness;*

2. *Harmlessness, truth, absence of anger, renunciation, peacefulness, absence of crookedness, compassion towards beings, uncovetousness, gentleness modesty, absence of fickleness;*

3. *Vigour, forgiveness, fortitude, purity absence of hate, absence of*

pride – these belong to one born in a divine state, O Arjuna!
(Bhagavad Gita 16:1-3)

The secret is in aligning to a higher vibration inherent within each positive quality. This process is called entrainment. Have you ever been in the company of those who drain you and leave you feeling weary? This is the negative effect of entrainment: to choose your acquaintances wisely as being around very negative people draws us down into a lower vibration. The same is true of aligning ourselves to those with a higher, spiritual vibration: we are drawn to vibrate at their level. Most people have so much internal chatter that they cannot hear God, that quiet voice within, speaking to them. Meditation is learning to listen in the deepening quiet for those soft approaching footsteps of God. When we align our thoughts on God by meditating on each spiritual quality or aspect of God, we become entrained to embody that higher vibration of the Divine Father or Mother.

Part 3

Meditations on the Twenty-Six Qualities

Chapter 1

Fearlessness (*abhayam*)

Fearlessness... is mentioned first because it is the impregnable rock on which the house of spiritual life must be erected. Fearlessness means faith in God: faith in His protection, His justice, His wisdom, His mercy, His love, His omnipresence. (Paramhansa Yogananada, *God Talks with Arjuna: The Bhagavad Gita* p. 956)

It takes a great deal of courage to face one's own inner samskaras or karmic issues. Through meditation, we can cultivate steadfast fearlessness. Our fears have kept us blinded lifetime after lifetime. Once we face these, instead of running away from them or avoiding looking at them, we find that they have no more power over us. They were just a figment of our imagination, with no more power than a puff of smoke. So, in developing a fearless approach to meditation, we learn to discern between what is real and what is unreal. Once you learn that the fear is not real, you quickly start to unravel other mysteries of life. It's as if you were asleep, dreaming that the landscape, peppered with pit falls and horrors, was real, only to wake and find that it was all a dream. Developing discernment of what is real and what is false quickly pans out into our daily lives as a result of meditation.

There are only two states of being: love and fear. Love only seeks to raise up and free that soul into bliss and ever-expanding light. Fear is the absence of love and can only see limitations. The 'what if ...' mentality will constantly jeopardise any escape from the downward, soul-sapping, spiralling trap of fear. All other negative emotions stem from fear, such as fear of rejection, fear of loss or death, or fear of fear itself. When we analyse any particular fear and peel away the layers of knots around it, we find that any fear of loss or rejection or even fear of being afraid itself, is simply fear. It has no power over you but that which you invest in it.

Fear of death is the greatest fear we can face. It is the fear of the unknown and fear of our own mortality. We have become so wrapped up in the illusion of our own story here on Earth, that we have forgotten our divine heritage. Fear of death is being afraid of the loss of body, loss of our accumulated possessions and loss of the people in the story of this earthly life. When faced with the mortality of the human body, most people will say that, it's only losing the people we love which matters the most. Although we never lose anyone whom we love as we are all One in spirit. At death of the physical body, most souls slide beyond the veil into their appointed place in the astral realm to be reunited with those we have attachment to. Death is just a transition between one state of being and another. Your place in the astral world is determined by the accrued weight of karma (payback from past deeds, emotional attachments or thoughts which is still to be redressed). Arriving in the astral world, under the loving support of your guides, we have a period of reflection as a re-run of the events of each life as to how successful we were in redressing the karma we incarnated to clear and that which would be in our best interests to face in our next incarnation. This is the cycle of birth and rebirth. We are bound into this cycle for as long as we identify with the physical body or our astral form. Meditation is THE route to withdraw from the unreal manifest forms and to realise our true nature which is boundless, formless, infinite spirit in endless ever-new bliss.

Fear of death occurs because we have simply forgotten where we came from and what we came for. We have become hood-winked to the wonderful bliss within that is our true reality. We have become like a beloved bird in a cage, which has become so habituated to its environment, it forgets that it once inhabited the open skies and soared free in spirit. In identifying with the human body as the only reality, it has become the cage of our spirit. Fear of death is a waste of time and energy as it is inevitable and only happens once in a lifetime, so we might as well get on with living now.

At some time or other on your spiritual path you will find yourself facing your mortality. A wise person will have prepared for the eventuality of the death of the physical body by weeding out any seeds of fear of death. At the time of your physical death, your passing in communion with God is also an important way to maintain fear-free thoughts and emotions as fear will only lower your vibratory rate, i.e. that you continue to vibrate at a higher rate whilst passing through the tunnel of death determines you a higher-realm astral world to inhabit for a while. The whole of the unseen cosmos is in a constant state of flow and expansion into higher and higher light consciousness. At the difficult trial of death your focus on God will elevate you to a higher state of consciousness.

You have a choice in any moment as to how you wish to be: to respond with love or respond with fear. Once you realise that life is only offering you two choices, that's a freedom moment. Life will continue to present you with more and more opportunities with which to respond, until you choose Love. In this book, we will explore how to choose the Love response to any situation which you find yourself facing, either externally or internally on your meditation voyage.

Exercise on Discernment of Love:

Write LOVE and FEAR on two scraps of paper and fold up the paper. Toss the pieces onto the table and select one at random.

Hold it in each hand. Close your eyes and feel into the word written on the folded paper. Is it light or heavy? Is it dark or light? Think of how this word makes you feel? Happiness or joy? Anger or sadness? Can you feel whether it is LOVE or FEAR? After a few minutes, guess the word which is written on the folded paper.

Unwrap the paper and note if your impressions matched the word.

Even thinking about the word Fear has the effect of shrinking and contracting our spirit, closing us inwards, bringing a state of alarm, the body starts to physiologically react as if there was a real danger. Love, on the other hand, has the effect of raising our mood, our energy, the light quotient of our auric field and a sense of connectedness and well-being.

In order to be fearless, we need to be grounded: connected to the earth we inhabit and to the incarnation which we are experiencing. Being ungrounded has a disconnected and not quite present feeling. Funnily enough, the process of becoming grounded and connected, involves trust. Letting go enough to become grounded involves the putting aside of fear and letting go in trust.

Remember, fear only seeks to hold you down and keep you back from your goal of enlightenment. It has no power to keep you afraid once you wake up to that realisation. Seen with the eyes of wisdom, fear has a valuable role in leading you to consciously realise that fear has no power, except that which you give it.

Prayer

Divine Father, teach me to discern truth from untruth and fill me full of your light so that I may fully appreciate Your Divine Will within all things.

This grounding procedure is the starting point for any of the meditations in this book. Through it, you will learn how to tune out the physical world and to quickly attune to your higher self.

Exercise: Grounding and Connecting to this Incarnation

Sit with the spine straight, close your eyes and sit quietly until you become present in the breath. Watch the soft inhalation and the relaxing exhalation. Become aware of any pauses between breaths. Without changing the breath, allow yourself to feel into these pauses.

Bring your awareness down into the tail bone. Become conscious of your breath making slight pressure changes in the tail bone against the seat on the inhale and releasing on the exhale.

Imagine that your tail bone doesn't terminate at the tip of the coccyx and that it has roots connecting down into the earth, flowing like hair or water. Your roots, connecting you deep into the earth: below building and bedrock and flowing towards the brilliant golden light at the heart of planet Earth.

This golden light envelops you in loving energy, washing clean all heaviness from your body. Feel that you are letting go of tiredness, physical and energetic toxins and all earthly difficulties. They simply flow from you as if you had turned on a tap. Mother Earth nurtures and heals us, transmuting stale energy into golden light. You may perceive the heaviness as treacle or tar. Keep breathing in softly and breathing out in gratitude, allowing yourself to release and let go until the flow slows or stops.

Then imagine you are bathing or swimming in this healing pool of golden light. Feel the golden light flowing up your roots and filling your body, as if it were hollow.

Visualise golden light flowing up and around the heart.

Golden light flows up through the head and out the crown to connect with a golden star above your head. Allow yourself to bask in this higher vibration gold light. Feel every cell of your body being healed, balanced and spiritualised.

Bring that golden light back into the heart. Be aware of being connected between the Earth and the higher realms.

Imagine golden light from the heart, flowing down the back, down the legs, under the feet, up the front of the body, over the crown, down over the back of the head, neck and shoulders. Be conscious that you are contained in a perfect golden sphere of light.

You are now ready for any of the breath practices (*pranayamas*) and meditations in this book. This is vital, as focusing on the breath is the bridge from outward identification with the physical form to the inner reality.

Pranayama: Ujjayi Breath

Ujjayi means 'victory from expansion'. This breath is used to direct the energy in the spine upwards to the brow (*ajna*) chakra. It is achieved by keeping the lips closed, opening the jaw to create space at the back of the throat and slightly contracting the glottis muscle in the throat. It's an exaggerated rasping breath, similar to slight snoring which sounds like 'haaaaa' in the vocal diaphragm and epiglottis. This breath rattles in the back of the throat, vibrating and calming the reptilian brain (base of the brain) which is involved with instinctual fight or flight responses. *Ujjayi* creates the expansion and upward movement of life force (*prana*) energy in the *sushumna* channel in the psychic spine. It's a soothing, calming breath which helps you keep your focus on the breath by listening to the sound it creates.

Once you are familiar with the basic format, we will bring in another level of focus: Earth breathing. This is done by physically continuing with *ujjayi* breath, as above, and bringing in awareness of breathing in unison with the Earth in this grounding meditation.

Earth Breathing Meditation (10-15 minutes)

Start by grounding into the Earth and attuning to the highest. Be conscious of being in a perfect bubble of golden light (above).

Bring your awareness to your breath using *ujjayi* breath. Feel into the spine as you breathe, imagining the spine as a hollow tube connected into the heart of the Earth.

Be aware that the Earth is breathing.

Imagine that the Earth is breathing through the hollow tube of your spine, as if you are a pore on the surface of her skin. That as the Earth breathes in, you breathe in. As the Earth breathes out, you breathe out.

Stay with this Earth breathing practice, using *ujjayi* to help maintain the focus. You may experience a cool wind blowing through the hollow tube of your spine.

Allow a detachment from the process of breathing, whilst still maintaining the awareness of being attuned to the Earth. The Earth is breathing you.

To close, become aware of your physical body sitting on your seat.

Be conscious of being in a perfect bubble of golden light.

Bring your awareness into your sitting bones and move the fingers and toes. Rub your hands together to create heat. Place the palms over your closed eyes and blink them open. Yawn and stretch.

Affirmation

I let go and deeply connect with my role in the Divine Plan.

Chapter 2

Purity of Heart (*sattva-samshuddhi*)

Blessed are the pure in heart for they shall see heaven.
(Matthew 5:8)

Purity of heart means transparency to truth. How many ways do we seek to conceal truth, even from ourselves? We prefer to project a squeaky-clean image of ourselves, often in the hope that we will believe it ourselves. Truth is at the heart of spiritual consciousness. 'If thine right eye offend thee, pluck it out.' As the Bible says, suffer not a stone to be overturned in your attempt to root out inner untruths. This involves us taking a discerning eye to our motivations: how and why do we respond to conversations and how honest are we in believing our own myths? Through practice, we can learn to employ our God-given discriminating intelligence (*buddhi*), rather than the mind (*manas*) and ego (*ahamkara*).

I'd like to take you back on a journey to an event in your childhood when you were dishonest. Perhaps you didn't own up to a fault and allowed another to take the blame for something which you did by saying nothing. Perhaps you verbally lied to stay out of trouble. Perhaps you lied to protect someone else. The event which comes to mind will be tinged with guilt, even though it was years ago, it will still come fresh into your mind and emotions as if it happened yesterday. The good news is you can release this now: Be honest with yourself about why you acted the way you did. You were only a child. Be understanding of the dilemmas and trials that faced you as a child. Can you respond compassionately to your inner child as if he/she were your own child? Imagine your younger self can off-load the guilt to you, your older self. Absolve and forgive yourself for the way

49

which you acted then. And ask yourself: what have you learnt from it?

You have the power to transform every wrong, or perceived wrong that you ever did just by acknowledging and accepting your motivations. Have the courage to put aside grudges and blame, as you observe yourself objectively in the mirror of truth. The more you move into transparency to truth, the clearer you feel. Choosing to develop purity works exponentially by transforming the heart, one shadow at a time. I suggest that you take time to explore transparency, placing each shame or guilt which was previously too painful to look at, firmly but kindly in your focus. You, the older wiser you, can at last see flawed thoughts, words and deeds as just the awakening process which you now find yourself within. Ask yourself: how could you know right if you had never experienced wrong? How could you know Self, if your little ego-self had never experienced other than Self?

Purity of Truth Meditation

1. Breathe in to the base of the spine. Be aware of an increase in pressure on the inhale, which can be felt in the pelvic floor. On the exhale, there is a release in pressure up the spinal fluid. Breathing works like a hydraulic pump: inhale creates a pressing down, exhale allows an upward release. Sit with awareness of this breath for 12 breaths.

2. Develop this breath by pulling up on the pelvic floor muscles (as if attempting to stop urinating) on the inhale, and release muscular control on the exhale with a sense of 'letting go'. Your focus should be with the increased upward flow of *prana*, or life force, in the spine.
Sit with this breath for 12 breaths.

3. Create the *jnanna* mudra by touching thumb and forefinger together on each hand, palms facing upwards. Sit with the

point of contact of skin on skin, forefinger touching thumb. Allow each point of contact to fill your entire awareness. Can you feel the centre of each point of touch? Can you feel something other than skin? This mudra completes an energy circuit for *prana*. You may become aware of the building of an intense light between thumb and forefinger on each hand.

4. Visualise a bright star on the brow and in the *jnanna* mudra on each hand. Linking each point creates an upward facing triangle. Sit with this awareness as you continue with this mental alternate breath practice:

    Start with your awareness on the point of contact of *jnanna* mudra on the right hand. Breathe in, tracing a mental line to the brow. Hold the breath and focus on the brow.

    Breathe out, tracing a mental line to the *jnanna* mudra on the left hand.

    Hold the breath and focus on the star between the left forefinger and thumb.

    Breathe in retracing the line from the left *jnanna* mudra to the brow.

    Hold the breath and focus on the brow, letting the light on the brow intensify.

    Breathe out tracing a line to the right *jnanna* mudra.

    Hold the breath and focus on the star between the right forefinger and thumb.

    Continue for 12 breaths with a ratio of 4:4:4:4 (breathe in for a count of 4, hold the breath internally for a count of 4, exhale for a count of 4, pause the breath for a count of 4). Only work on the ratio of the breath if you are able to maintain the focus and do not become breathless or your breathing becomes ragged. Work up to being able to maintain a ratio of breath, prior to that just work on the energy links between the points of the stars in this exercise.

5. After 12 breaths, let the breath focus go.
   Mentally connect the lower points of the triangle between right thumb and forefinger, and left thumb and forefinger. Breathe into that connection, increasing the light. Breathe out, releasing the energy to intensify in each hand.

6. In the star triangle between brow and each hand, breathe in the quality: *Purity*. Breathe out, release through all three points. Focus on maintaining your focus in the centre of the triangle, the heart. Breathe in *Purity*, letting go on the out breath. Continue for as long as you can maintain focus.

Prayer

Divine Father, illuminate my being with your presence. Clear all impurities of spirit that I might love thee with all my heart and soul.

Chapter 3

Steadfastness (*jnana yoga vyavasthiti*)

If we could arrive at these Mansions (elevated spiritual levels) by letting others make the journey for us! That is not possible, my sisters, so, for the love of the Lord, let us make a real effort.
(St Teresa of Avila, *The Interior Castle*, Dover Press, p. 43)

Spiritual perseverance in seeking wisdom is essential for the liberation of self-realisation. I teach many students how to train their minds, firstly, to concentrate with single-pointed focus (*dhyana*) and then to meditate on achieving divine union. The universe is stacked in your favour as a beginner in meditation. Early on, the majority of beginners experience the calm, mental quiet, greater control and heightened consciousness that meditation brings, if they put in the practice. However, after a while, the early flashing light display on one's mental screen, the calm or bliss may become less obvious. Sometimes the person becomes bored once they realise the considerable mental effort and persistence that is required to progress in meditation.

A dogged, stoic approach reinforced with a well established meditation routine is essential. A frequent internal mental display confirming that something is happening just because you are meditating becomes a less regular occurrence over a period of time. One must at some stage persist in spite of the lack of obvious signs of progress. At this point, the dedicated meditator learns to proceed with faith alone. Perhaps you may experience sporadic heightened experiences, or perhaps not. But do not be deterred from your goal of self-realisation.

Many are called but few are chosen (Matthew 22:14).

Persistence is one hallmark of most enlightened beings. They have sat for considerable periods in inner silence to build the ability and stamina for their brain and body to withstand the incredible power of light of a Self-realised master.

By way of encouragement, I would say, a job sooner started, is sooner finished. I like to use the analogy of a cairn. Each attempt to sit in meditation to unite with God is like placing a pebble on the cairn. It doesn't take long to create a sizeable mound. Obviously, if you choose to meditate twice a day, the mound grows quicker. If you meditate for longer and deeper periods, it is as if you are placing huge boulders on the cairn. Over several years, you will have a veritable monument as a testament to your commitment to your goal of Self-realisation.

I use this analogy to illustrate that, even when you think nothing is happening in your meditation practice, in the absence of any obvious signs of progress, I assure you that you are in fact preceding towards Self-realisation. Incredible visions and light displays can be experienced as markers of early progress but then these can become a hindrance. Many choose to become stuck at the level of the astral realm and to be mesmerised by shiny baubles such as greater psychic and mental powers. In effect, they are replacing one *maya* or illusory reality for another. Seek to ignore any displays on the screen of the mind as a distraction to your progress. Look deeper. Look beyond those illusions. What's behind them?

Question: who is the 'I' that is having the experience? Observe that you have an outer face and an inner face (that is acceptable to yourself): an inner dialogue that is between you and not you. The real you is neither the outer face (physical body) nor necessarily the inner voice. Are you looking at the Self or an aspect of the little ego-self? Seek He who made you, the unchanging Self. Peel away the layers of not-Self to reveal Self.

Knock and the door will open, seek and ye shall find. (Luke 11:9)

Steadfastness is then a noble spiritual quality. My friend, I beseech you to keep on, keeping on.

Prayer

Divine Father, lead me to experience your presence within every breath and to find your heart beating within my own heart.

Pranayama: Viloma Pranayama

This breath, teaches us to extend the exhale. As the inhale is active breath, we can tend to be more aware of the act of breathing in. *Viloma*, meaning opposite, is an interruption to the natural, unmonitored flow of the breath. *Viloma pranayama* helps us to develop control of the breath flow and is an easy method of learning to extend the exhale and increase the spaces between the breaths.

The physical breath, in this body bag of bones, can be laboured at times. Viloma *Pranayama* guides us to find a refinement in the physical out breath and develops spaces between the breaths where we can experience freedom from the mechanical process of breathing. This is not to say that the breath is held unnaturally but that in the pauses between the inhale and exhale, we can experience absence from physical body awareness. In the pauses in the breath, a magic happens. We find a lightness and joy as we can discover God-consciousness behind the breath.

Meditation: Deep Earth Connection & Alignment to the Highest Light

Perceive yourself as seated in the centre of a yellow square, like the foundation of a pyramid. Become aware of the solidity of the stone beneath you and its stability.

Imagine a golden channel of light extending down from your tail bone, through the square foundation, connecting with the golden light at the centre of the Earth.

Concentrate on letting go through many layers of your being (physically, mentally, emotionally, letting go in trust) into the golden light of the Earth.

Experience being welcomed into the golden light and be aware if any layers of resistance arise within you.

Mentally affirm: *I let go in complete trust.*

You will know when you are aligned and connected with the Earth when you feel an answering response of golden light flowing upward towards your heart space. Allow your heart to be bathed in golden light.

Breathe in pure white light and visualise breathing out grey impurities to any trees near you.

Continue to consciously breathe in white and out grey for 12 breaths. Notice that your connection with the earth through the golden rod of light deepens with each breath.

Visualise a golden stream of light upwards from the heart and out through the crown of the head.

Consciously connect to a higher and brighter light than you've previously done. Allow your consciousness to sit within this white star of light as if you are being purified with each breath.

Consciously breathe in the pure white light of the star and concentrate on being spiritually purified with each exhale. Continue for 12 breaths.

Bring your awareness down into the middle of the head.

Imagine that you are sitting in a channel of light (*nadi*) between the brows (*ajna chakra*) and the back of the head (medulla oblongata). For this awareness, raise your consciousness from the two physical eyes, to the astral awareness of a sphere of light displayed on an internal movie screen between the brows.

Practise *ajna* gazing into the spiritual eye (irrespective of whether you experience light or not). The important aspect of this practice is the steadiness and persistence by which you gaze internally at your own screen.

Finish by visualising the golden rod of light between heaven and Earth.

Let healing power flow to the Earth.
Bless all beings on the Earth.

Affirmation

I awaken into awareness of Divine Perfection.

Chapter 4

Charity (dana)

As you give ,so shall you receive.
(Luke 6:38)

In the beginning, God being One Spirit, created the many as reflections of His Omnipresence. So that He could experience being One in many, and many in Oneness. We, as expressions of the One appearing as many, are still in our hearts irrevocably linked as One. God makes no separation or division between the lowliest creature or the highest spiritually vibrating being in his Creation. All are meted equal divinely apportioned unconditional Love, no matter whether we remember God as the heart of all things continuously, frequently, sometimes or never. That is Divine Love in action. Divine Love seeks no blame or judgement, although karmic law ensures that just results are in operation as a counter balance to thoughtless, harmful thoughts and deeds, in order to point us in the right direction: the inward focus to reunite consciously with God who is continuously singing our praises in love and devotion that we may remember our way home.

Viewed from this cosmic perspective, other beings are simply expressions of the One, clothed in bodies which serve the cosmic illusion of separateness. Know that at the very heart of our being, we are One in spirit. This is the realisation that awaits you in meditation. Intellect based 'knowing' viewed from the limited stance of the human mind cannot comprehend that. This is a flawed vantage point, as the mind cannot encompass anything greater than itself. But from the cosmic perspective, which we share equally in our hearts, we are One. This truth is universal, whether we know it consciously or not. God maintains that truth and continually upholds us in His Divine Love, patiently waiting for us to realise this truth from our delusional perspective as separated from God as many bodies; angel, human, animal, plant or mineral. We still are One.

How then, can we realise the truth of separateness as unreal? This is where karma yoga comes in. Karma is interpreted here to mean 'taking action'. As we sit within our body-bound isolation from each other, it is through generous, selfless actions (*seva*) that we reach to connect with each other.

Each thought, word or action is marked as creating karma for us, unless it is totally unselfish in nature. Through karma yoga, we can work out karmic debt and become free of the wheel of life and death, birth and rebirth.

We give because we see ourselves reflected in others: the same God spark within each and every one. God spark shines brighter in those who develop self-realisation through meditation and through acting selflessly. One acts because our divinely given hands, heart and head can be used to express our spirit selfishly for ego demands or selflessly as agents of God. Choosing to act as if we are expressing God's Will, instead of the ego's small will, illumines both our spirit and those whom we offer our services.

Lord, make me an instrument of your peace,
Where there is hatred, let me sow love;
where there is injury, pardon;
where there is doubt, faith;
where there is despair, hope;
where there is darkness, light;
where there is sadness, joy;

O Divine Master, grant that I may not so much seek to be
consoled as to console;
to be understood as to understand;

to be loved as to love.

For it is in giving that we receive;
it is in pardoning that we are pardoned;
and it is in dying that we are born to eternal life.
(Prayer of St Francis of Assisi)

St Francis' prayer is one of the most beautiful expressions of handing over ego will and acts of charity as surrender to God's Will. Here is expressed a model of living truth: that we can serve God which we can see behind the pain or joy which we may witness within the eyes of our brothers and sisters on this planet.

Practise first and foremost, giving the greatest gift to God: your love. All other works of charity will flow from the nectar of this divinely-ordained gift. If God is continually giving wholly of His Self and you realise that you are perpetually basking in His Divine Blessing, what greater gift can you give than to bestow this blessing on others as a conduit for Divine aid? Like the 'Little Drummer Boy', learn to offer whatever you do well, as an act of service to the Lord. It is not the big, showy, ostentatious displays of benevolence but the smallest acts of kindness that can make the most difference in the eyes of God.

Not all of us can do great things. But we can do small things with
great love.
(Mother Teresa)

Sometimes, when another is experiencing such acute suffering that they will not accept help, it can be difficult to witness their suffering. Know that at these times, when we are perhaps feeling helpless, that as our heart goes out to them in compassion, we have given our love. The power of prayer is always at our disposal. Prayer is a direct appeal to God for intervention and succour to alleviate their suffering. To see divinely, is to realise that we are One in spirit, with the same hopes and dreams, and need to love and be loved in equal measure. If you are unsure what to do to help, ask yourself: how would God want me to act? Begin the process of Divine charity today, by extending the hand of friendship towards your fellow brother or sister in spirit through action, blessing or prayer.

Uttarabodhi Mudra: Gesture of Enlightenment

Thumbs touching and extended, index fingers steepled (extending away from the body) and all other fingers clasped loosely. Place your hands gently in your lap.

This mudra charges us with pranic energy and inspiration.

Pranayama: Breath Observation

The breath will be our vehicle of service in the following meditation. Sit quietly, bringing your observation to the inhale in comparison to the exhale.

Do I naturally give or take through the inhale?

Do I naturally give or take through the exhale?

Meditation: Giving of your Highest to God

Sitting upright, visualise a lightning rod of white light from above the head, down the spine and into the pure, white star in the centre of the earth. Discharge all negative mental and emotional charge into the earth.

Visualise white light travelling up the spine to the navel chakra: charging the navel with pure white lightning.

Visualise the white light flowing upwards into the physical heart, over-spilling and flooding into the lungs: charging with life-giving light.

Visualise the heart chakra as a radiating, beautiful pink flower of unconditional love. Rotate the heart chakra 90° on the spine to face upwards in the spine. Beam your love upwards in the spine towards God.

Visualise the throat chakra as a radiating, beautiful blue flower. Rotate the throat chakra 90° on the spine to face upwards towards the crown chakra. Let your heart's love pour through the head.

Visualise the top of the skull opening, like a sunroof, into the lotus of the crown. Offer your heart's love of God to flow into the petals of the crown.

Let your heart's love be so great that it flows beyond to higher realms above the head.

Let your love be a fragrant offering at the lotus feet of God.

Prayer

Divine Father, I open my heart to express thy love.
Divine Mother, I see your beautiful eyes looking out behind the suffering in all souls. I open my hands to deliver your love and blessings.

Chapter 5

Control of the Senses (*dama*)

Consider purification (tapas), which literally means 'to melt', as in refining ore. The purpose of purification is not pain or penance, but to deliberately refine one's life, to melt it down and recast it into a higher order of purity and spirituality. The goal is very important: it is not self-punishment but refinement to shift from human existence into Divinity.
(Jack Hawley, *The Bhagavad Gita: A Walkthrough for Westerners*, 17:14)

At some point on your inward journey, you will be challenged to resist temptations and desires brought about by the senses. In a physical body there is an innate tendency to seek out experiences which give us pleasure and to avoid those which give us pain. Throughout life in the physical world, we develop successive conditioning of learned behaviours where we seek to maximise pleasure and minimise pain. While this animalistic trait can be seen to have relevance in helping us avoid dangers to our physical health or survival, such as being cautious with fire, fear of exposure to the danger can lead to excessive avoidance or phobias.

In this chapter, we will be exploring self-restraint by replacing bad habits with more spiritually beneficial habits. With the onset of good vibrations from regular meditation practice, old habits of over indulgence and indecision are conquered. There is no need to directly focus on eliminating bad habits as these will naturally fall away as the good habits supersede them. Remember too, that *anything which you focus on increases*. This is Divine Law. So that, if you focus on bad habits, even with a good healthy intention to eliminate them, this will have the undesired effect of manifesting or magnifying these habits. Therefore do not dwell on bad habits, simply change your focus to the acquisition and establishment of helpful ones.

Just as you would most likely perform your morning rituals in an order, plan a routine which will help you to adopt a good habit like a ritual. For instance, if you want to commune daily with God, establish a firm time to meditate, even setting the alarm clock so that you put your most important relationship, with God, first in the day. Do not put off to tomorrow that which you can do today. The longest path, after all, begins with the first step. It takes 6-8 weeks to establish a firm habit of constant repetition. Put it in your diary or schedule planner if needed or place post-it notes at strategic places to remind you to stay on track, until the habit comes automatically. When a good habit is firmly established, to forget to do it would be as unsettling as forgetting to wear underwear or leaving the house without your mobile phone. You just won't feel right without it.

Ultimately, adopting better habits will be nurturing and fill us full of well-being, until such times as that habit is no longer needed. See all habits as a mode of interaction within the role we find ourselves in on this planet, which, as we incrementally release our identification with our human part in this earthbound drama, habits just fall away when they are no longer needed, the nearer we are to the ultimate goal of *Samadhi* or God-consciousness. As this occurs, all need for other props or support from habits is eliminated. In *Samadhi,* there is simply God-bliss. Nothing else exists and the yogi then realises that all of creation, including good or bad tendencies, are simply reflections of the One Divine Consciousness and that nothing exists outside of this Ever-new Bliss of the soul in Oneness.

However, I would caution the meditation student not to dispense with good habits too readily. See it for what it is: ego identification. If you have not experienced God Bliss as a full-time soul experience, then the Quiet Inner Voice of conscience will guide you in maintaining and upholding good God-habits.

I would like to tell you a story here.

Once upon a time there were three little boys who wanted to go into space. The first boy read story books every night and never stopped dreaming of being the first man in space. The second boy quickly tired of dreaming of being an astronaut and moved on to dreaming of being the fastest racing driver. The third boy was fascinated by flight, created a model aircraft club at his school and went on to be a pilot. Which one do you think went into space, the one who dreamed and stayed true to his dreams or the one who acted out his role? Very often children still have a fresh perspective and memory of their life purpose for this incarnation but somehow along the way, they can get sidetracked when the road proves harder than they imagined it would be but those who have the courage to act on their convictions are more likely to succeed. The answer is that the third boy manifested his dreams into reality and in 1961, Alan Shepard Jr. became the first American man in space and later became the fifth man on the moon.

Whatever you align yourself to, you will manifest. This is why establishing and routinely maintaining a meditation practice will eventually lead you to your goal of enlightenment. It takes the physical action to manifest this process; otherwise it will remain just a thought process. In this physical world, in a physical body, we are required to act: to maintain this body temple and to fulfil our duties, and act as an agent of the Divine, uplifting our brothers and sisters on the planet.

It has been said by ancient sages that the path of Self-realisation is as fine as walking the blade of a knife: to think, say or act with attachment to an outcome becomes a bondage to the karmic wheel of birth and rebirth. We, over time, learn to monitor not only our words and actions, but every thought. Meditation gives us the tools to slow down the thought processes until we can catch a thought before it has the energy to arise and to ignore it. All thoughts may seem to be unstoppable or irresistible to our curiosity, just a juicy bit of gossip we can indulge in, turning over and over trains of thought which, when we suddenly become conscious of what we have been doing for the last ten minutes, we realise we had got carried away on the thought-train. In starting to learn self-restraint, we learn to detach from the stream of thoughts. Observe that there is a spaciousness to disengage from the mind's content through each un-pursued thought as it percolates past. We learn to discern whether this is worthwhile, following it to a helpful conclusion. We learn to ignore unhelpful thoughts. These may appear to be thought bubbles effervescing up from old patterns of behaviour or emotions, lodged mainly in the three lower chakras, as if they are at the sides of our vision. In order to let the old patterns go, we learn to hold our attention fixedly ahead, instead of 'looking' at the thought. Know that thoughts cannot exist without your attention. If you can hold your attention on something else for 2 seconds, the thought will have passed on by. Let me reiterate the power of will that you have: if you maintain your thought focus on something else for 2 seconds, undesirable, unheralded thoughts will simply cease to exist. Isn't that freeing? Only 2 seconds of focus is required.

When the attention is drawn to the outer body-shell, our vital force (*prana*) is distributed unevenly across the body according to where we place our attention in the body. Our senses continually send us messaging about the external world which we can choose to listen to or respond to. Ultimately, it is a choice whether we give in to fears or desires. Sometimes these can present themselves enticingly as being all pervading. Have you ever been so overwhelmed with desire or fear that you are rendered useless to think clearly? In those moments, we can become so swept away with passion (positively or negatively), that the passion becomes all encompassing. It's as if you are caught up in a horrible nightmare that you are powerless to wake up from.

I wish to remind you here, that you have a choice. When

passion sweeps you off your feet, remember you have a choice. When fear comes knocking in the dead of night, remember before you get carried away in your own drama-dream that you can pull it back into evenness. Think of a moment when the world threw you some lemons and you smiled and carried on regardless. Choosing to not react to dramas that are present in your life, you will develop stamina and strength to face all that life could fling at you. So, like the proverbial phrase, the next time life hands you lemons, learn to make lemonade! You have the power within you to create the life experiences you find yourself facing.

We can learn to withdraw the life force from the five sense organs, of smell, taste, sight, hearing and touch which keep us materially focused. Feedback from the senses can be so alluring and attractive that we seek to replicate pleasures again and again. As you have no doubt discovered sense pleasures are so transient and momentary, they're here and gone like a firefly in the night. So why are we so tied into them? The answer is that the feedback from the senses lets us know where we are in this physical reality. We have forgotten that there is another mode of being. We have forgotten that we are actively, moment by moment, creating the external reality through our thoughts and attachment to actions. We have forgotten what it felt like to not be in a physical body and how freeing and expansive that felt. The human body is heavy and gross in relation to our spirit self; every breath takes great effort as if we are breathing with a boulder on the chest. But we are used to the heaviness and learn to distract and entertain ourselves with trivialities because we forget that we once knew lightness of being and boundless joy in life. Third dimensional reality kind of pulls the wool over our eyes and blinds us to the truth of who we are and how powerful we really are, unless we meditate. In meditation, we shut out the messages coming from the body, constantly informing us of where we physically are and what's going on around us, in favour of uncovering the truth of existence as inner peace and deepening bliss.

A Personal Mantra

I would like to introduce to you how powerful it is to use a personal *mantra*. A *mantra* can be a mentally recited phrase with a specific intent of aligning you energetically to an enlightened master, time-honoured spiritual ritual and awakening spiritual insight. Mantras are the repetition of words and phrases of special significance, and can be said either out loud or internally. All of the spiritual paths have some version of mantra. Mantras which have been used by millions of people have a well established vibration signature within the energy grid of the planet which you can readily tap into. By saying a mantra you are connecting to the energy field of all those who have also used that mantra before you. Powerful examples are:

Aum In Hinduism, this is the sacred sound within creation. It's the extended sound of *Om* and is said to mean, It Is, Will Be or To Become. This is the 'Amen' of Jews and Christians and the 'Amin' of Muslims (see chapter 15 on AUM).

Om Mani Padme Hum Tibetan Buddhist mantra meaning *'Hail the Jewel in the Lotus'*. The Buddha of Compassion is the sacred jewel.

I am that I am From the Hebrew Torah, when God gave Moses the name of God.

So Ham The Hindu mantra, meaning 'I am THAT'.

The secret in establishing a *mantra* is to select one that you resonate with and to keep using it and not to be tempted to switch mantras. The divine knowledge contained within that mantra will unfold for you in a series of insights over time. This will not be apparent straight away, but stick with it and not only will you receive intuitive insights but a spiritual strength. The mantra will become a rock for you, a firmament when all of the rest of your life seems in chaos, either externally or internally. It is particularly beneficial when you are in a period of emotional upheaval.

The mantra, taking us into the present moment and beyond the ego, slips through the narrow gate into the city of God. (John Main, Benedictine Monk)

How Do Mantras Work?

A common theme in spiritual traditions is that the universe began when God created sound.

In the beginning was the Word, and the Word was with God, and the Word was God. (John 1:1)

In the beginning was Brahman with whom was the Word, and the Word is Brahman. (Hindu Rig Veda)

Mantras are a way of introducing and focusing this vibration, or original sound, in ourselves.

Sound is a form of vibration and everything in the universe vibrates at a certain frequency. When we repeat a mantra, we align with the vibrational frequency of that mantra, so that we too begin to resonate with the vibration or key energy signature of that mantra. By saying a mantra you are literally tuning yourself to resonate at the same vibrational frequency as God, the healing power or the intention of that mantra. With practice, as you come to resonate at the same frequency as the mantra, the mantra gains its own momentum. Then, *'you stop doing the mantra, and the mantra starts doing you'*.(As in Sufism).

Many mantras work on the mind-body connection by creating a biofeedback loop that replaces unpleasant sensation with love and positivity. The subsequent reduction in stress and anxiety can have innumerable physical benefits. Most of us have experienced being caught up in a repetitive pattern of thoughts. When these thoughts are negative or angry this can be particularly unpleasant and often damaging but replacing these with a mantra, we not only break the habitual negative flow, we also create and reinforce a new flow that is both beneficial and positive.

It's not necessary to investigate the old thoughts, simply replace them with a mantra.

Recent studies into the neuroplasticity of the brain show that neural pathways are either strengthened by repetition, or weakened by lack of use. We learn to associate positive emotion with reciting a mantra. The key is in 'catching negative emotion' and transferring instantly the positive emotion that you normally associate with the mantra.

If find yourself stuck in a downward, emotional spiral, a mantra can break the emotional pattern and replace it with the positive emotion that you normally associate with the mantra. As soon as negative thoughts arise, you learn to replace them with a mantra. You are literally rewiring your brain whilst simultaneously weakening habitual thinking. It takes surprisingly little time to establish that level of pattern, like a song that gets stuck playing over and over in your head, a mantra becomes second nature. Your mantra is with you all the time. You could be washing, cleaning, driving, walking or waiting in a queue but it's always there for you to draw on. My mantra used to kick in when I was carrying a heavy bag of groceries in rhythm with my footsteps or when executing a physically demanding task in rhythm with my breath and helped me focus peaceably on something other than the strain. It was also wonderful in the dentist's chair, giving birth or during unpleasant hospital procedures. I found it personally at hand with any challenging situation in life and no one knows that you are using it. It's a quiet strength and inner relationship with God that you are instilling, one repetition after another, one step at a time. Deep-seated tendencies, *karma*, and impressions derived from past experiences, *samskaras*, can be altered and erased by the continual contact with the energy of a mantra. Mantra is a powerful tool to use to transmute and clear karma.

Mantras work on a different vibratory level to affirmations. Affirmations work on the psychological and emotional level, which can be very useful, but mantras work at a deeper spiritual level. A healing affirmation can establish the specific intention to be healed by manifesting the vibratory power of the words. This works by programming the mind to manifest a state of being and, while very powerful, it has a specific ego-driven intention. Mantra, on the other hand, works on a level high above the mind, has no limitations and expectations except spiritual unfoldment and alignment with higher vibratory consciousness.

How to Establish a Mantra

Establish a mantra in a quiet meditative space. Take a few deep breaths and still yourself. Place your focus on your heart or between your eyebrows as you use the mantra.

If your mantra is associated with a deity or master, visualise the energy connection as you say your mantra.

It is easy to be distracted and think of something else, even while you are saying your mantra. It helps to repeat the mantra aloud to establish it. As with any other meditation practice, if your mind wanders, firmly and gently bring it back to the sound of the words or the resonating effects within the head, throat, chest or abdomen.

Mala (rosary) beads can be used to count the number of repetitions, using the sense of physical touch, and to send back messages to the mind to remain engaged in the process. As the energy of the mantra builds, you find yourself carried away into a timeless space outside the experience of everyday linear time. Time flies when you are so much in the moment. It's very freeing.

Nadi Shodhanam (alternate nostril breath)

This breath is important as it balances the right and left side of the body and brings you into calm in the centre. It also activates the brain and attunes the brainwaves to a longer, slower rhythm. Physiologically, it's great for relieving migraines and sinus congestion. *Nadi shodhanum* performed consciously over a period of time clears and purifies the subtle energy body, *nadis*, fibre by fibre.

Basic format – Stage 1

Sit with the spine upright. Be aware of the chin being level. Experience how adjusting the level of the chin slightly allows or closes the flow of *prana* in the spine. Focus on allowing maximum flow of light into the head.

Place your dominant hand over the face. Thumb on one nostril, two smallest fingers on the other nostril. Tuck the index and middle finger into the palm. Experiment with lightly pinching just below the bony cartilage of the bridge of the nose. You can open or close each nostril, thereby focusing the flow of the inhale and exhale through one nostril at a time.

To start: breathe in through both nostrils. Breathe out through both nostrils.

Close the right nostril; breathe in through the left nostril. Pause the breath and hold the awareness on the brow chakra.

Close the left nostril; breathe out through the right nostril. Pause.

Breathe in through the right nostril. Pause with the awareness on the brow chakra.

Close the right nostril; breathe out through the left nostril.

This process constitutes one round. Repeat for 12 rounds.

Prayer

Divine Father, free me from restlessness and reveal Your perpetual peace within.

Chapter 6

Sacrifice (yajnas)

As the heat of the fire reduces wood to ash, the fire of spiritual knowledge burns to ashes all karma.
(Bhagavad Gita 4:37)

Yajna means a purifying ritual or sacrifice with spiritual significance as an offering to God which dissolves ego attachments. We are tied to the cycle of death and rebirth by three *gunas* (*Guna* literally means 'strand of cord or rope') by our selfish attachments to desires and to the outcome of our actions in this earthly realm. Until we can learn to let go of our attachments to sense gratification and our actions, we remain bound to this cycle. A clue that you are not free is that you have been born in a human body, unless you are an enlightened master, here to remind us of our heavenly station and not to accept anything less.

The three *gunas* or delusive states of Cosmic Nature, *tamas, rajas* and *sattva,* keep us bound to the karmic cycle of bodily death and rebirth. Until we can learn to transcend the human experience beyond bodily consciousness and activity, we remain mired in *maya (cosmic illusion)* by the three *gunas. Sattva* is the positive tendency towards good: truth, purity and spirituality. *Tamas* is the negative tendency towards darkness: untruth, inertia and ignorance. *Rajas* is the neutral but activating quality which creates constant activity as it works on *sattva* to suppress *tamas* or vice versa. At any moment, we are constantly under the influence of one or another guna, until we learn to turn our mind and will beyond these to God. Any action performed under these three influences with attachment to the result or to restless inclinations (ego), causes karmic bondage.

Throughout the day, the dominance of each of these states ebbs and flows within each person. We are constantly weaving attachment to the karma of our own lives. Through the three coloured threads of Cosmic Nature, we are engaging with the narrative around us: white (*sattva*), red (*rajas*) and black (*tamas*). Some say that an enlightened master can look down the length of your lifeline and perceive which thread was predominant at any moment; how well we remembered our divine mission in this incarnation or became fogged in delusion will be recorded on our *akashic* (soul) records. The majority of people are in the *rajistic* sphere, acting selfishly in the world but this is the testing ground for the soul. Eventually, people are drawn to act benevolently. However we are still tied to the karmic wheel of birth and rebirth until we can learn to perform our daily activity for God, with no thought of ego attachment.

Obviously, to do kindly tasks for others within this world demonstrates a higher state of being than the person who operates *rajistically* and selfishly just for themselves. However, the *sattvic*, benevolent, person could still be attached to achieving happiness ('I do it because it makes me feel better') or praise ('I do it because I am liked') or attached to knowledge ('I do it because it makes me spiritually proud and powerful'). We must diligently guard against long-forgotten karmic traits of *tamasic* (non-virtuous) behaviour sub-consciously lurking behind even virtuous acts. Don't be surprised when, in meditation, these traits arise from the depths: in the process of releasing the unreal, veil after veil, non-virtuous feelings or memories are revealed. These long hidden leviathans of past lives can be released if you consciously realise that no one is judging you and that you have been choosing (subconsciously) to hold on to the rope of attachment. This is the freedom moment. Release attachment by letting go of the rope tying you to that negative characteristic. These are revealed to you when the time is ripe and you have the spiritual composure, will and strength to let go.

Over a period of years of meditation, increasingly finer and finer discrimination of what is Reality and what is non-reality develops. Who is the 'I' experiencing this? Is it 'I' or ego?

The fire of cosmic consciousness consumes all binding, stored-up karma. Unlike the ordinary person, the self-realised master does not have to reincarnate. She has dissolved from her mind all restless agitations, desires and delusions. She realises that her body, mind and spirit are gifts from God. She owns nothing. Even her soul belongs to God. She has transcended the physical and astral realms and knows that God is the sole-doer of any action. When she acts or speaks, it is from the realisation that it is God who performs the action, God who speaks from these lips and God's Will that she has been given bodies to don to perform in the world at all.

Purifying Exercise

In this exercise, we will be recognising, plucking out and banishing any unwholesome character traits that have been revealed. Sitting quietly, recall a negative trait which you have noticed is blocking your inner peace. Write the quality on a scrap of paper and fold it. Lay it aside until the end of this practice (no psychoanalysis). This will be used in a fire rite to purify your *samskaras* (karmic traits).

Kappalabhati Pranayama (shining skull breath)

In Sanskrit, *kapal* means 'cranium' or 'forehead' and *bhati* means 'light' or 'perception and knowledge'. Thus, *kappalabhati* is the breath which brings a state of light or clarity to the frontal region of the brain. It is a cleansing practice which invigorates the whole brain and brings subtle perception and insight, which should be performed on an empty stomach.

Kappalabhati breath also activates the fire centre at the navel (*manipura* chakra) by way of a rhythmic pumping of the diaphragm. In a normal breath, the inhale is active i.e. the diaphragm is pulled down to draw air into the lungs, and the exhale is passive i.e. the diaphragm simply relaxes to push the air out. In *kappalabhati*, the opposite is true. To exhale, we forcibly contracted the lower abdomen and pelvic floor muscles like a pump and the inhale is passive, drawing air into the lungs by a reflex action.

Sit with the head and spine straight. Rest the hands in *jnanna* mudra (thumb and forefinger touching).

Close the eyes and relax the body. Inhale fully through your nose.

Exhale through both nostrils with forceful contraction of the abdominal muscles.

On the in breath, allow the abdominal muscles to relax and breathe in passively (naturally). The in breath should be a spontaneous recoil, with no effort.

Complete 10 rapid breaths.

On the next 2 breaths, inhale and exhale deeply and fully twice. This is one round.

Take a few normal breaths. Practise 3 to 5 rounds.

Caution: if you become light-headed or dizzy, stop and build up your stamina slowly. Kappalabhati should never be performed by those with a hernia, heart disease, high blood pressure, epilepsy, pregnancy or a stroke.

Purifying Meditation

Ground into the golden light of the Earth through all four petals of the base chakra *(muladhara)*. Envisage connecting through a column of white light extending from the spine in the centre of the base chakra, into the earth.

Consciously release your chosen negative trait down in this column of light to be transmuted and purified by the golden light of the earth.

Then bring golden light up the column and spine into the heart: golden light circulating around the heart. Take this golden light into the head and out through the crown to connect with the highest purest light above your head. Visualise being bathed in a shower of this high vibration light which cleanses away any debris of the negative quality from your auric field.

Bring the higher light down into your heart and place yourself in a bubble of purifying golden light.

Quietly, consciously focus on offering the quality to God for release on the out-breath. With wisdom you realise that this trait is not you. Experience a sense of gratitude that at last you recognise what is true and what is false.

Replace the vacuum this quality once occupied with pure, white light.

Allow a state of grace to descend, lifting you into a higher state of being. Sit with grace for a while.

Finally complete the rite with a physical ritual. Burn the piece of paper in a spirit of offering and reverence (outdoors, ensuring that there is nothing flammable nearby). Make a prayer of gratitude as you watch the paper burn, knowing that the last vestiges of the trait have been purified.

NB: this is a very transforming, deep practice which may leave you in an altered space for a few hours. Factor in time to sit and reflect quietly afterwards and drink plenty of water.

Even if thou art the most sinful of all sinners, yet thou shalt verily cross all sins by the raft of knowledge.
(Bhagavad Gita 4:36)

Prayer

Divine Father, help me to realise that I do not act, it is You. Lift me from ignorance into wisdom, suffering into bliss and restlessness into acceptance.

Chapter 7

Study of the Scriptures (*svadhyaya*)

Right study of the scriptures leads to emancipation. A true devotee does not suffer with mental indigestion as does one who gorges himself on scriptural lore without understanding its meaning and without assimilating it into his life.
(Paramahansa Yogananda, *The God Talks with Arjuna: The Bhagavad Gita*, p. 959)

Scriptures from all religions are a direct download of codes through a saint or master detailing how to live a godly life and how to seek God-realisation or union with God. Study or chanting of the scripture which you are drawn to, will help you unfold on your spiritual path. It can also help you to identify and weed out ungodly behaviour patterns or thoughts, thereby illuminating the inward Godly path and lead you to Self-realisation.

The vibration of the written word on paper has an effect on our energy field, whether we are consciously aware of it or not, either to raise or lower our frequency, depending on the spiritual level of the writer. When we read scriptures, we tap into the frequency of the master who received the words as a direct communication from the Divine. This process is called entrainment. At the opposite end of the spectrum, you can lower your vibratory rate by reading violent or trashy novels, newspapers or magazines. It is a mark of your spiritual progress when the desire to read such material simply falls away. In comparison to the bliss achieved by entraining to a higher vibration, old habits cease to attract you to fritter away your existence on tittle-tattle and gossip. Don't beat yourself up if you still occasionally read material which you know, in your heart of hearts, isn't wholesome or spiritually advancing: when the time is right, the feel-good factor of higher vibration practices, will become so alluring that the latter will be released without effort.

Some spiritual seekers voraciously read New Age spiritual books, devouring second-hand wisdoms. True knowledge comes firsthand and internally arises as experiential truth. Seek to cease browsing and skim-reading a breadth of spiritual books without ingesting the kernel of truth contained within. It is better to dig deeply than to dig up the whole beach with shallow holes. It is a mark of your growing wisdom, when you learn to be discerning in your choice of reading material. Place one hand over the cover and 'feel' if that book has something to offer you spiritually. Allow your intuition to guide you and you won't need to even open the cover.

Over time, you may find that your need to read diversely falls away in favour of the work of a Divinely Illuminated Master. Through the process of entrainment, we link directly with the magnetic illumination of the Master by carrying that intention while reading his or her words. Seek to dive deep into one chosen text, being ready to peel back the layers of knowledge it contains. Intellectual understanding is not true divine knowledge. This takes patience to open your inner core to reveal the secret. Repeatedly 'knock at the door' until you are answered with a sudden earth-shattering illumination: that is deep spiritual wisdom. Do not be satisfied with anything less than that.

Spiritual teachings can also be received just by opening the book. This direct download of the seed of wisdom by God's grace, is called *shaktipata*. One such moment of grace arose within me when I opened a book on Kashmir Shivism devotional teaching by Swami Lakshman Joo. It was as if a golden light came from the book and enveloped me in a state of bliss which lasted for days. Thus, I know the power of a scriptural text to uplift and transform to a higher spiritual realm, sometimes without even having to read it. When I started reading the Bhagavad Gita, I would 'ingest' the Sanskrit text, in such a fashion, knowing that on some level beyond mere human intellect I was able to comprehend at a soul level.

Reading religious scriptures for understanding is vital as the teachings and kernels of truth which you uncover will be assimilated into your life. Most scriptures are written in code. It isn't intended that the insincere reader will learn the truths it contains without a level of personal commitment and attainment. Direct appeal through prayer to God and meditation is the process by which the secrets contained in code become clear. Then the wisdom becomes experientially, super-consciously realised. It is important that there is a direct connection between you, the process of learning and what you are reading, then, that truth becomes such an integral part of your being and so becomes an unshakable bedrock of stability in your life.

Entering into every heart, I give the power to remember and understand: it is I again who take that power away. All the scriptures lead to Me: I am their author and their wisdom.
(Bhagavad Gita 15:15)

Know that there are many learned people who profess to know the deep secrets within religious texts from an intellectual basis but who do not live this truth. Without the life-changing epiphany of deeper insight of intuitional knowledge, intellectual knowledge itself is worthless. Intellectual knowledge can provide a guiding philosophical skeleton and framework upon which one can chart a clear, tried and tested path forward in spiritual life, but it is secondary to awakening insight and inner growth. I urge you to be discerning when listening to those who pontificate but do not walk their talk. Discernment is a hallmark of spiritual wisdom. As a rule of thumb: if you feel bombarded, then it's likely to be an ego driven discourse, no matter how elevated the religious personage may seem. Your gut feeling will let you know. Seek instead to know spiritual truth by your own right study through prayer and meditation so that you directly internalise the teaching. Most prayers are appeals for something material without any real belief in receiving and, as such, are less likely to be responded to.

> *Every begging prayer, no matter how sincere, is self-limiting. As sons of God, we must realise that we have everything already that the Father has.*
> (From *Whispers from Eternity* by Paramhansa Yogananda, 2008, Crystal Clarity Publishers, Nevada City, California)

So, pray to God for illumination, read the passage twice and then sit quietly in meditation and wait for the inspiration to come. That state of quiet expectation is living in the moment, each minute pregnant with the possibility that, in that moment, your prayer will be answered. Rest assured that all sincere prayers for God-realisation are heard. Your role is simply to fine tune your receptivity or hearing, if you like. By this process, meaning in illumined texts is gifted as a firsthand revelation into your soul as true wisdom.

Select a scripture that your soul feels drawn to through higher wisdom of intuition.

Pranayama: Nadi Shodhanam

Focusing on the breath will help us to raise our soul vibration to a state of receptivity conducive to selecting or meditating on a scripture. We will revisit *nadi shodhanam* with a new focus as a tranquilising breath which balances and harmonises the two hemispheres of the brain. *Ida* and *pingala*, two main *nadis* (psychic energy channels) on either side of the spine are brought into balance and *prana* is encouraged to flow through the spine. This is conducive to divine illumination and insight in the centre of the head.

Hold awareness in the brow (*Ajna*) chakra as you practise

nadi shodhanam, with hands placed as in stage one (see p. 45). The breath moves towards the brow on the inhale, hold at the brow on internal retention, breath moves away on the exhale. Allow the pivotal point to be the brow. Do not follow the journey of the breath, merely find it arriving and exiting the brow. (In this way we learn to focus on the breath but will eventually perceptibly shift from the physical breathing to the breathing *prana* (life force); all of the exercises in this book will intensify detachment from the physical as a subtle and developing journey.)

Stage 2: Repeat for 12 rounds, counting the breath, aiming to lengthen the exhale and internal retention.

Inhale	Hold	Exhale	Hold	
4	4	8	4	for 4 rounds
4	8	8	4	for 4 rounds
4	4	8	4	for 4 rounds

Then, maintaining awareness on the inside of the brow, chant OM aloud. Focus on the vibration of the sound: chest; throat; back of the throat; back of the skull; facial bones; brow.

Sit quietly in meditation on the brow.

Meditation: Brow Temple for illumination of scriptural texts

Visualise a delicate flower, petals glowing in a light of their own. Become aware of its alluringly sweet perfume which draws you closer to receive the blessing of its scent. You are drawn deeper into the flower until you are sitting inside the centre, surrounded by the walls of the petals shining in a heavenly light of their own. Sit quietly, allowing your spirit to become one with the flower temple around you. As you concentrate on the heavenly aroma, your vibration is raised. You and the flower temple shift into a higher state of being.

Ask for illumination and the blessing of understanding the scriptural passage you were reading. Sit in silence with an air of expectation.

Allow the silence to be so profound that you can hear the vibration of the petals singing. Then you are receptive to hearing.

Allow the silence to be so profound that you receive understanding instantly in a flash of intuition so that you just know beyond words.

Sit with the expectation that your prayer is answered.

Be patient. Meditate on one scriptural passage daily for a week. Be open and receptive to receiving the kernel of truth after meditation in the form of a message from a stranger, tuning into nature or a chance reading of a book. For whatever you are currently concentrating on will also be evidenced in the outer world if you are perceptive.

Prayer

Heavenly Father, Divine Mother, reveal thy mysteries to me.

Chapter 8

Self-discipline (*tapas*)

The Supreme Reality stands revealed in the consciousness of those who have conquered themselves. They live in peace, alike in cold and heat, pleasure and pain, praise and blame.
(Bhagavad Gita 6:7)

God has given us free will to stay true to our spiritually homebound path or to be swayed from this course by a myriad of desires and attachments. In being seduced from the path, we can forget the knowledge that: that which we align ourselves to either becomes our bondage or leads us to soul freedom. That is to say ego-driven choices born from unchecked passion, sloth, greed, hunger for power, envy or anger etc. will incur a karmic debt. On the other hand, benevolent actions, thoughts, and words incur little karmic debt. There is nothing that is done, said or thought under the sun which does not have its equal and just consequence unless it is offered up in genuine renunciation to God (see chapter 13). Thus bad habits and even good habits for the benefit of our brothers and sisters on this planet, all incur karma which ties you to this wheel of birth and rebirth. Obviously, there are degrees of karma and adopting a good or better habit is a step in the right direction towards enlightenment and freedom from bondage to continuous rebirth. The long term spiritual goal is to relinquish all habits and ties for Unity in Spirit.

In this chapter, we will learn that by practising self-discipline, we can learn to withstand bodily discomforts such as cold and heat without mental fluctuations. We will also look at our inner desires and fears and how both extremes lead us from the path of non-reaction and mire us in the lure of the physical world.

Through self-discipline, we can learn moderation in all things, which is the Path of Wisdom, including: celibacy or sexual moderation if you are in a relationship; restraint from eating (see chapter 17, absence from greed); and to withstand extreme heat or cold. The aim in self-challenge is to loosen up the ties of attachment to bodily comfort. Attachment to the narrow confines of warmth, shelter, food and sex keep us bound to bodily awareness. It is necessary to break beyond those confines in order to experience soul bliss. Note your reactions, if any, to the suggestions in this chapter, they may reveal some insights about body attachment to sensation.

When I was undertaking my yoga teacher training course, I was encouraged on several occasions to move beyond the narrow confines of my comfort zone and challenge myself with actions that I would avoid for fear of discomfort, such as taking a cold shower. Just think about that one – if you are already a convert you'll know the stimulating benefits, but if you haven't, just note the aversive reaction which you experience at the mere mention of 'cold shower'. It sounds like a punishment. Why on Earth would anyone subject themselves to that torture? I'll answer that one for you. Firstly, as a test of inner strength to see if you can knowingly step forward into a cold spray. Hippocrates purported that water therapy 'allays lassitude' (physical or mental weakness). Secondly, as a tool to cleanse the auric field of mental and emotional negativity which I find useful when you feel contaminated by proximity to others' emotional garbage. Thirdly, cold water hydrotherapy is an effective treatment for depression and other mental disorders because wet and cold causes our surface vessels to vasoconstrict (tighten up) making blood move from the surface of the body to the core, as a means to conserve heat, which reflexively bathes the brain and vital organs in fresh blood bringing nutrition, oxygen and gently detoxifying the area, enabling the brain to 'reset' its neurotransmitters. Lastly, and most importantly for the spiritual aspirant, you can develop spiritual stamina when you learn to keep focused on your inner soul sanctuary and become remote from reaction to the physical response to the cold water. If what you focus on increases, can you place your attention on mental calmness, not reaction? If you focus on the body reaction to cold, it will gasp and complain. But there is another way. If you develop *indifference* to bodily discomfort, and keep your consciousness in an inner calm, you learn that you can control *mental* fluctuations. The body will still automatically react but if your attention is not in the response, you can tune out discomfort. How powerful is that?

If we can learn to tune out small discomforts, then we have the power to tune out reaction to body injury or illness. Would this be a healthier mode of being when faced with unavoidably challenging situations in life? That's when your spiritual training comes to the fore and you realise that you have the inner strength, stamina and unaffectedness to cope with all life throws at you. So, the next time that you bump into something through no fault of your own, note the reaction arising to body hurt: anger, injustice, blame throwing, nursing the hurt to obtain sympathy etc. We learn to transfer the spiritual stamina developed through training e.g., indifference to cold water. Through such practices, we are adopting indifference to circumstance. Although, we should use common sense to avoid harming the body unnecessarily as, for this incarnation, it is our god-given body-temple and should be respected as such.

Another self-discipline challenge might be to religiously practise an *asana* (yoga posture) barefoot on the grass for 108 days, rain or shine, or recite a *mantra* 108 times for 108 days. The dedication and self-discipline required to commit to a practice for a length of time is very revealing and exposes hidden aspects of our inherent nature. There will be many times when the challenge seems insurmountable but you don't need to travel to Nepal. You can climb your very own Everest which, although it may not be publically acclaimed, will be ultimately much more spiritually satisfying, especially if you make it a sacrifice of ego to God.

I once undertook to prove my spiritual intention to God by vowing to perform a daily Yoga Four Directions sequence barefoot on the grass for 108 days. Like all pilgrims, my own personal Camino Way journey started with the longest step: contemplating the commitment. The challenge seemed easier when I had begun, although the first rush of enthusiasm is soon thwarted when inclement weather sets in. As rain is a fact of life in Scotland, I set my collar to the drizzle and got on with it. Pleased with myself for having got over inner resistance to getting wet, I found that it was actually pleasurable. Screwing up my face and anticipating distaste were unnecessary reactions. Somewhat pleased with myself, I felt fortified to stay the course. However, greater inner challenges were in store. Just when I was getting into an enjoyable daily rhythm, life threw me a curve ball. My downstairs neighbours' back bedroom overlooked my tiny backyard and once they had discovered me, the strange, lanky woman upstairs, waving her arms around in bare feet, I became the daily sport. I must have been a remarkable sight! Having set out to overcome reaction to public embarrassment and to erode ego-self-consciousness, ironically, the universe went to town on challenging me! Every day the neighbours stood at the window, 12 feet from me and pointed, laughed and shouted. It was daunting but luckily I was already in a comfortable rhythm with the cool, soothing grass, the flow of the sunlight on my arms, the concentration on the breath and offering peace to the spirits of the North, East, South and West. I found that it was relatively easy to tune out the unpleasantries and connect to my inner centre. My staying power proved to be greater than my neighbours', who with no reaction on my part, gave up eventually. In fact, the whole process was so cathartic it became the foundation of my spiritual commitment in a day.

Even though, I continued through, rain, hail, snow and frost on grass, I learned a stoic tolerance for temperature and took such an inner strength from the experience that I continued for another two months after the target date.

So what is the significance of 108? Research into the mystical number 108 reveals some very interesting insights, namely: there are 108 *nadis* (energy lines) converging on the heart chakra; each angle in a regular pentagon is 108°; there are 108 Upanishads (ancient wisdom texts). 108 is a power number. A string of *mala* beads has 108 beads and is used, like rosary beads, to mark the number of repetitions of a *mantra* or prayer.

I would invite you to select a spiritual practice with the spirit and intention of a personal offering to God. All of the practices mentioned in this chapter are carefully selected from time-honoured traditions which I have experienced as personally beneficial.

Pranayama: Bhramari (Humming Bee) Breath

Sound is a great focus. It links us into our throat chakra whereby we can hear the Inner Voice of Truth speaking in our heart. This *pranayama* will be used as a meditation to align us deeply to that Inner Voice through deeply listening to the humming sound in the throat. The Humming Bee breath also resonates through the reptilian brain at the back of the skull. The reptilian brain deals with our fight or flight reflex and is constantly searching for danger to react to. The Humming Bee breath quietens the brain stem, sending soothing vibrations and calming the nerves into deep safety and security. In this state, we can effectively listen to our inner voice which is usually drowned out by too much over-stimuli from a constant state of vigilance for external dangers.

Performing *Bhramari* deeply, reassures us that we are always safe and that nothing can rock us from internal security and calm, unless we choose to let it influence us. We can build on this internal security so that we can learn to disengage from over-identification with perceived threats and maintain an internal calm, no matter what might be happening externally. I say this to encourage you to continue on the inward path, but not to be discouraged when this does not happen overnight. Then you will understand the need to establish and maintain good God-habits until such times.

Practising *Bhramari* involves vibrating the throat by humming quietly with lips closed, teeth separated. The tongue is pressed lightly against the roof of the mouth, which shifts the resonance to the nasal cavity.

Sit quietly, with the spine upright with hands in *jnanna* mudra.

Concentrate on deepening the in-breath in the throat by using *ujjayi* breath. You may feel a cool breeze coming up the spine to the back of the head.

Hold the inhale and focus on the spiritual eye on the brow, inwardly chanting *Om*.

Raise your hands to the ears, pressing the ear flaps closed with the thumbs. Hum continuously on the long exhale, vibrating the throat.

Feel the hum vibrating throughout your brain.

Repeat the sequence 5 to 12 times, having one or two normal breaths between each *Bhramari.*

Meditation on the Inner Space

Sit in silence. Allow the sound of the breath to be your complete focus.

If thoughts intrude, pay them no attention.

Learn to train your focus by pausing the breath until the thought passes by unhindered. Even a flicker of attention will amplify and expand the thought.

Let the sound of the breath become so enthralling that each part of the breath is an ever-renewing experience.

Become aware of the start, middle and end of the inhale –

maintain focus for the full inhale.

Allow the in-breath to be suspended in the air, like a ball thrown upwards hanging smoothly in its parabola as if frozen in flight, before it softly starts to descend into the exhale.

Maintain focus for the beginning, middle and final puff of the exhalation. Become quietly observant of any part of the exhale where your attention might wander. Become extra vigilant in the next breath.

Can you maintain focus for one full inhale, pause and exhale without a flicker of inattention?

Ride the pause between breaths with intense attention and suspended thought interference. Open up a space in the centre of the head, where only white space occurs. Hold the pauses in this space.

Allow the eyes to remain immobile behind the lids. Use inner focus to gaze softly ahead into this white space.

Thoughts may percolate past but do not intrude without attention. Nothing exists except white light, gaining in intensity with each focused breath.

Affirmation

I am One, I am not this body. I am awake and aware in God's love. I am One, I am God. I am God, I am One.

Chapter 9

Straight Forwardness (*arjavam*)

Tell the truth boldly, whether it hurts or not. Never pander to
weakness. If truth is too much for intelligent people and sweeps
them away, let them go; the sooner the better.
(Swami Vivekananda)

The eyes of God see within each one of us all lies, hidden agendas
and grudges nursed in secret. We may think that we can fool
others or, in vain, try to hide truths from ourselves but we cannot
fool God. In our hearts, we are as if transparent crystal. Every lie
etched in dirty marks, hidden agendas emblazoned in neon and
every grudge we hold onto besmirching our inner glory.

The clearer we become when practising deep meditation,
devotional prayer to God and breath practices, the more
obvious any dishonesties become to ourselves. It will feel tight
and uncomfortable in the heart. We can only close off petals
in the heart to hide the truth from ourselves for so long. Many
incarnations ago, you may have been so hurt that you have
maintained a hard-done-by feeling of being wronged. You may
have learned that by telling lies, you were able to save your own
skin but we carry the scars of each ill grudge and untruth in the
heart chakra. You may have been so hurt that you have tried to
protect yourself from more pain, by closing down the petals of
the heart, but as you become lighter, it hurts more to be closed.

In this chapter, we will be tuning into our own hearts. The
heart, being halfway between the ego-bound desires of the
lower three chakras and the heightened spiritual unfoldment
of the higher three chakras, is pivotal in bridging into higher
consciousness.

Take a moment here to close your eyes and scan into your

heart chakra. Visualise the 12 petals of the heart lotus. As you feel into each one, register if any are closed of tightly folded in. Do you feel equally open on both left and right? Does your heart feel tight or painful? If the answer to any of these if yes, how long do you think that you have been like this? Does breathing into the heart help it to open or does it remain closed?

By way of healing our heart space, we will be using all that we have learnt about holding awareness and intention to deepen into a healing meditation for each petal of the heart in turn. I have listed these below as 12 separate clearing meditations in their own right, with the final meditation building unity, transparency and love as a bridge between Earth and your heart role in this present incarnation.

To start each mini-meditation, quieten the breath and tune into your heart chakra. Feel, see or visualise it as a shining green lotus-like flower, pulsating with light in response to you tuning into it. Imagine each petal like the twelve points on a clock face opening out from the centre. Start with the first petal meditation at one o'clock, second at two o'clock, third at three o'clock etc.

Heart petal 1: Commitment to Opening to Life

How much on a scale of 1-10 are you committed to opening to life, warts exposed and all? The affirmation 'Feel the Fear and Do it Anyway' stems from this heart petal. Let go of reservations so that you can commit to being open no matter how many times you many have been hurt, to remain open to trusting the process of life. Know that you are always supported and that your guardian angels and guides hold you in a space of unconditional love. Nothing that you could have done or said would cause them to judge you and find you wanting. God only wants the highest good for you. It is only in retrospect that we realise how much a seemingly challenging change turned out to be a blessing in disguise. What if you open up to life *always* presenting you with a blessing in disguise? We need not be so cautious and cagey. Trust your inner discernment from the 'sounding board' in the belly, your inner sense of knowing when something is right or wrong for you. You can trust that you will always become alerted by inner knowing so that you can open to meeting all life challenges with an open heart. *I open to all that life brings me with an open heart.*

Heart Petal 2: Happiness

Happiness is our God-given natural state. How much do you embody happiness? Open this heart petal to letting the quality of Happiness be expressed by God through you.

My well-spring bubbles over with happiness from the centre of my being.

Heart Petal 3: Tender Motherly Love

This petal links with the Divine Mother's deep love. Our birth mother may have fallen short of the perfect Mother. Let any ill feeling go. Step back so that you can recall that she was also tied to the karmic wheel of birth and rebirth and learning how to live from the highest. Release past memories and in prayer, connect with the Divine Mother's perfect love as she tenderly holds us close like an infant child. Imagine being cradled and having every need catered for. Divine Mother will pick you up before you can fall. Imagine what it feels like to cradle a baby bird which has fallen out of its nest or a newborn animal and learn to extend that protective, tender love to your own heart. Imagine cradling your heart in loving hands which the Divine Mother is working through.

I am cradled in the arms of the Divine.

Heart Petal 4: Integrity

Sticking to your truth, even in the face of adversity, builds a magnetic integrity of spirit. The path of truth is often not an easy one. In past lives, we may have a soul memory of being punished or killed for speaking the truth which makes us reticent to place ourselves in the line of fire. However, fear not and let the past fall away. In meditation, turn your focus inward into this heart petal. 'Charge' it up with integrity which in turn delivers strength of purpose. Keep breathing spiritual strength into this petal until you can 'see' it shining bright as a shield of light. Once open, this petal will stay open offering its spiritual shield of encouragement for the opening of the whole heart.

I am a spiritual warrior standing for truth and light.

Heart Petal 5: Innocence

There is strength in softness, in a child-like, feminine quality. In the face of persecution, we may have learned to be hard line. We may have been told that showing any softness was a weakness, like exposing our vulnerable underbelly to the wolves. Ask yourself: would you rather be a wolf dominating others' weaknesses? Or do you project that you'll always police your boundaries to protect your own vulnerabilities? Can you conceive of dispensing with wolf-like hunting or a fear of prey mentalities? Both are based on fear. In adopting Innocence, we allow the walls to come down. Visualise that Innocence exudes such a deep bubble of acceptance for all that is around the heart, that only love can exist here. Imagine beholding the world as if through the eyes of a child, every moment unfolding with a magical effervescence. Imagine connecting with a fairy or riding a unicorn. Imagine your heart with the softest of rose pink petals, exuding a rose perfume as it opens to the morning sun. Innocence allows us to be as a little child living in glory.

Suffer little children to be unto me.

Heart Petal 6: Inner Strength from Loving Unconditionally

Each heart petal, as it opens, leads us ever inward in a spiral to the centre of the heart rose. Learning the lesson of loving unconditionally, we move from loving with ego-based love that loves to be loved or for personal benefit, and into Universal Love. Our perspective pans back, and from this higher vantage point we can see our brothers and sisters throughout creation as individual drops of the same vast ocean of consciousness. Seemingly separate in an illusion of duality: there's them and there's me. As you tune into petal six, let pre-conceived notions of separateness fall away. Learn to love God like you have never loved before. Our premier relationship is with God. It is by loving God that we learn to love others, realising the same God-light within each being that you meet. God loves us unconditionally with the perfect unwavering love, no matter how we might stumble. When you pray to God for illumination and love Him with all your heart, this petal becomes as strong and burnished as beaten metal shining in the sunshine.

I am loved unconditionally and through my love, I set others free.

Heart Petal 7: Sweetness from Lack of Guile

Each thought and heart emotion creates a perfume in the ether around us. Hidden agendas and lies leave a bad taste in the mouth. Is this petal exuding a sweetness like honey? Or a sourness like wine? Subterfuge and attempting to keep guilty or shameful secrets hidden, causes this heart petal to close in tightly as if to cover the secret from prying eyes. Know that there are no secrets from God and, in truth, there are no secrets which you can bury out of sight from yourself forever. Feel into this petal: is it robust? Or brittle, threatening to shatter into shards of ice dropped on the sidewalk? Did you consciously make a vow or pact with God to keep the secrets hidden? How much inner peace does this petal carry? Or is it crying out to release the burden of a terrible secret? How much are you able to conceive of energetically letting go of the burden? Or would you rather take this weight to the grave with you? Know that we are all subject to the laws of karma and in reality, that burdens are carried into the next incarnation for release and justice. In the light of karmic truth, visualise handing over heaviness within this heart petal to God. Lay all your troubles and vows at the feet of God. Keep letting go until God's mercy fills this petal with the sweetest intoxicating perfume, filling the whole heart.

I am bathed in the sweetness of God's mercy.

Heart Petal 8: Letting Go of Loss or Regret

In the beginning of all time, we knew a purity of Oneness as sparks of eternity expressed as individuals blissfully singing the One song of creation. This heart petal holds the heart's longing to be back in bliss and unity. No matter how many pathways we have travelled in error, seeking that Oneness with the Creator, your inner longing is calling us home. Learn to let go of regret. Regret holds no soul purpose but to hold us back from blissful immersion in the whole. Loss and grief for people or place are false expressions of self. Why would God allow us to suffer? Is it, in fact, we who perpetuate suffering though identification with this physical reality? Everything on Earth is subject to change. It is easier to accept the tide will always flow than to fight futilely against it, like King Canute. Imagine breathing into this petal with the rhythmic flow of the ocean. Allow your little wave to join the ocean, wherein abides all those who you may have lost. Become one with the ocean of peace.

I am as One in God's Ocean of Peace.

Heart Petal 9: Delight and Child-like Joy

How many times has your heart felt stuck? Frozen in space, in time, in hurt? Our natural state of being is in soul bliss in Oneness with the whole of creation. Think back to a time when you were carefree, usually as a child. For this heart petal we are going to tune into a remembered state of joy and delight and amplify it throughout the whole heart. Remember the sun shining as you played, oblivious to anything except your Joy of being in the moment. Feel it. Allow your lips to smile. If you want to laugh, or sing or dance for joy, let that full uninhibited expression of self come through. Learn to tune out self-consciousness or hurt. Replace it with your innate natural state. Keep feeling, visualising and smiling into that joy-filled delightful snapshot of time and space until it expands into present time and space. Know that Heaven can be here on earth. It is not sometime in the future or after the transition of body-death. It can be here and now. Heaven is a state of Being and what you create life to be.

My life is filled with never-ending Joy and Delight in living.

Heart Petal 10: Reverence

God holds our consciousness close to Him and upholds our perfection for now and ever. It is only we who have turned away, seduced by earthly pleasures and forgotten how blissful it is to be in accord with our heavenly father. Every time we think 'God', we can re-forge that soul union when we mentally say it with heartfelt longing and reverence. Imagine God were not in a distant heaven or time, but residing in your heart. You need only turn inwards to your heart cave, where the flame of Spirit burns unceasingly and connect. Talk to God as your dearest friend, father, mother or lover. That secret relationship in your heart of hearts is always open to you. God will never judge us. We only turn away when we have judged ourselves harshly. Remember Innocence (link with petal 5). Build a strong inner connection by dialoguing with God in your heart. He is the perfect Father figure. She is the perfect Mother. God loves us without question. Come into a quiet meditation in the stillness, visualise entering your heart cave and lay down your life for God.

In bliss I am upheld in God's Love and my soul flies free into the arms of God.

Heart Petal 11: Transparency from Fear

Feel into this heart petal. Is it tight or open? Tightness reveals that you have reacted by recoiling in fear when you were hurt of threatened. Fear always causes us to close down, limiting our soul expression and shutting us off from soul Oneness. Seeking to be safe from harm, when we have shut down our heart, has the exact opposite effect of causing us to feel unsafe. Choose to unfold this petal. Tell your inner child that they are safe. Keep breathing into this petal until the tight grip of fear lessens and is replaced with a transparent lightness of being. Banish all fear. You have nothing to fear but fear itself. Visualise a clouded glass petal and each conscious breath clears the frosted glass into transparency.

I let go and reveal in my inner soul all God's Glory.

Heart Petal 12: Completion and Maintaining the Whole

In the beginning was the word and the word was God. In petal 12, we come full circle: the Alpha and the Omega, the first and the last. We uphold the completion of creation within our own heart. A radiance of petals shining in Glory, bask in your inner light. Charge this petal to hold the maximum charge of Light. In visualisation, let the light from this petal spill over into all the other petals in sequence until all are brimming over with Light. Feel the expansiveness in waves flowing through the heart petals. Maintain a continuous circle of light until each petal unfolds to become part of the Whole.

In Inner Peace, I carry the balance of creation in my heart of hearts.

Chapter 10

Non-harming (*ahimsa*)

The key message of *ahimsa* is to live our lives without causing harm to anyone, any being or to ourselves. When Paramahansa Yogananada in his '*Autobiography of a Yogi*', asked the great master of non-violence, Mahatma Gandhi, about his definition of *ahimsa*, he said it meant: '*The avoidance of harm to any living creature in thought or deed.*' There you have an indication of how far reaching and impactful *ahimsa* is as a way of life. On a path of ahimsa, not just every act but every word and thought is self-monitored as to whether it could actively or potentially cause harm to self or others.

In this chapter, we will be eliminating actions which cause harm in ourselves, our inner relationship with God and to others. In meditation, we will be clearing harmful thoughts at source and filling the void with good will to others or God's Will.

When I was a child, Kingley's '*The Water Babies*' was highly influential to me. Tom the chimney-sweep is taught many lessons on moralistic living by aptly named characters, of which my favourite was Mrs Do-as-you-would-be-done-by. This became my self-check before acting: would I like this done to me? If not, I tried to choose a better response. Later, when I was 12, there was a phase when students concealed dressmakers pins on the underside of their blazer lapels which they used to jab each other. Most people joined in, I suppose in the mistaken belief that in so doing they could protect themselves from being terrorised. I refused to follow that regime. Being vocal in pointing out that I was doing nothing to harm my attackers largely had the effect of me being left unmolested. My motivation wasn't cowardice. I strongly believed in acting from conscience; my rule of thumb came into play. I would not do to others what I wouldn't like done to me. It was pretty nasty to be on the receiving end so why would I want to do that? I wanted to show by good example how it was possible to walk the path of pacifism in the dog-eat-dog baptism of fire which was a Scottish secondary school.

The Old Testament, an eye for an eye, sheep-mentality is hard to understand. Gandhi once summed it up when he said: *'An eye for an eye ends up making the whole world blind.'*

Without conscience, that inner voice of knowing the right path to take is to act blindly. It seems to me we must move beyond that feeling of hurt. 'I hurt, therefore I will make you hurt', has perpetuated so many poor practices across the world but it heartens me on social media to hear of unremarkable individuals from all cultures performing remarkable actions to change our world for the better. Then you realise that the buck stops with you. It's not up to someone else to do the right thing. That task is down to you. Whatever you find yourself facing in life, the challenge is to have the courage to take the path of non-violence, not the path of least resistance.

I'd like to tell you a story here.

There was once a wandering Buddhist monk who had very few possessions, relying on his faith in God to provide for all his needs. Being very pure and holy, he lived a life of non-violence and was well-respected by villagers on his travels. One day, he arrived at a village which was being terrorised by infamous bandits. As the raiding hoard came riding into the village, the people hid and cowered in fear. The monk remained where he was in the centre of the street, as the fearsome war-chief approached brandishing his sword.

'Get out of my way,' bellowed the war chief, with blazing eyes. 'Don't you know who I am? I could run you through with this sword!'

Unperturbed by this show of violence, the wise man calmly replied, 'Don't you know who I am? ... I could let you.'

This story always fills me full of shivers. Which one is acting from a place of inner strength? The holy man is so full of God-consciousness he does not experience any duality between living and a bodily death. He knows that body-death is just the transition into another state of being and that the soul continues unmarked.

The soul cannot be cut: it cannot be burnt or wetted or dried. The soul is immutable, all-pervading, ever calm and immutable: eternally the same.
(Bhagavad Gita 2:24)

Reflection:

Is there something you are avoiding, even though you know it is the right thing to do? Explore your motivations for resisting acting from conscience. Is there a life challenge in this obstacle which you recognise is a common pattern?

Do you harbour any ill will in thought towards others? Make a commitment to take to task all slacking as regards avoidance of gossiping and malicious thoughts towards others. Can you recall any incidents when you succumbed to gossip? Did it make you feel powerful or leave a nasty taste in your mouth? True power comes when we have the strength of character resist harmful words erupting from our lips and remain in silence, rather than polluting the ethers with poisonous vibrations. No wonder it leaves a nasty taste to speak ill of others, living or beyond the veil.

Do you beat yourself up mentally? Thinking destructively is to place a barrier between you and your inner connection with God. Ahimsa sets the balance right and builds a bridge of inner connection at soul level. Many of us have become accustomed to the dulling down of life in the fast lane in modern city/town life. Concrete jungles disturb our inner connection with all that is. Out in nature, we remember the inner connection with all of creation and how good that feels. We remember to be kinder, more compassionate and not violent to self. Once we stop the inner fight, as if the universe were against you, we start to realise our place in Unity. *Ahimsa* builds that bridge. Destructive thoughts erect barriers between you and God. Destructive deeds are also a futile method of distancing ourselves from that which scares us.

Pranayama Viloma Anuloma (cutting the breath)

This breath is intended to develop a finer quality in the breath and to extend the exhale. Destructive thoughts and emotions can overlay the breath, if we so choose to let our emotions run away from us. This colours our field of consciousness (aura) in a constantly changing display of lights, darker colours for a darker mood, bright colours for loving emotions, etc. It is important to not only keep the full attention on the breath but to focus on refining the out-breath so that we breathe the fine quality of non-violence into our bubble of light or *prana* bodies that surround the physical body.

Start by sitting comfortably with the spine upright, chin level, shoulder blades towards the spine. Focus on the exhale to lengthen it and bring your attention to it, *'feathering'* the out breath to be as soft as possible (see chapter 3).

Gayatri Mantra

The *Gayatri* mantra (pronounced 'guy-a-tray') is a devotional prayer for light and illumination from the ancient Indian scripture Rig Veda (10:16:3), which is chanted or sung to attune us with the *Aum* vibration. It builds a very powerful sound vibration to tune us in with God through the sound of creation at the centre of our being.

It is beyond human competence to describe the glory of the Gayatri. Gayatri is the primordial mantra that destroys sins and promotes wisdom, and nothing in the world is more important than wisdom. The Gayatri Mantra has specifically manifested so as to destroy falsehood and establish truth.
(Adi Shankaracharya)

The Gayatri has three parts: first as praise of the Divine; then as a reverential meditation; finally a prayer of appeal to the Divine to awaken to Universal Reality.

It transforms us from the everyday humdrum into pure alchemy of sound and being. The Gayatri contains all the important Sanskrit seed sounds (*bija mantras*), each syllable perfectly balancing and attuning with the alphabet of which is said to be the oldest, purest root language on earth. Try listening to a recording online to help with the pronunciation and join in. Once you have the metre and rhythm, focus on the syllables resonating within you as you chant or sing. When you have learnt it mechanically, tune in with the devotional heartfelt praise in the *Gayatri* as it transforms into a deeper connection with God.

Oṃ bhūr bhuvaḥ svaḥ *Ultimate reality, in which physical, astral and causal worlds exist,*

Tát savitúr váreṇyaṃ *That is the supreme reality from which creation happens, and is the foremost,*

Bhárgo devásya dhīmahi *O Divine Effulgence we meditate upon you,*

Dhíyo yó naḥ pracodáyāt *Propel our knowledge of the Supreme Reality.*

Of most sacred verse, I am the Gayatri.
(Bhagavad Gita 10:35)

Earth Grid Meditation

This meditation amplifies the quality of *ahimsa* or non-violence within the crystalline grid structure of Earth so that all beings can more easily tap into the new paradigm for living on this planet.

Once you have 'feathered' the exhale to cleanse, soften and release the fibres of karmic attachment and raised the soul vibration by chanting the *Gayatri* mantra, then you are more receptive to tuning into your higher purpose here on this planet.

Connect with the Earth by grounding down to the golden light in the centre of the planet via roots from the tail bone.

Maintaining a steady focus on the inhale and exhale, from the vantage of the middle of the head, start to bring awareness into the energetic spine as a hollow tube of white light. You may be aware of *prana* or life force moving in the spine with the breath.

Breathing in: *prana* moves upward in the spinal column.

Breathing out: *prana* moves down to the base of the spine.

Visualise the seeds of the chakras as vibrating colours in the shaft of the spine.

Know that your seat of consciousness can travel up or down the spine, just like travelling in an elevator.

Visualise travelling through the shaft of light into the base chakra, where the shaft continues down into the heart of the Earth.

Focus on the four petals of the base chakra and visualise them rotating upward in the spine.

Visualise rising through the column of light into the centre of the head. Gaze calmly towards the brow chakra which has two cool petals. Take your breath into softening these petals, left and right.

Be aware of the column of connection between the base and crown chakras. Focus on the breath moving *prana*: up on the inhale; down on the exhale.

Focus on the heart chakra in the centre of the column of light. Keep focusing on the breath practice for several minutes as if you are breathing *through* a soft, all-loving heart.

Continue this practice until the power of love in the heart for the Divine and all beings everywhere builds. You may experience the heart chakra rotating 90^0 to face upward in the spine, beaming love and compassion into the petals of the crown.

Let your awareness sit within the lotus of the crown. Become so bright that the light spills in rays from your head. Continue the breath focus and intensify this breath on breath.

Visualise the crystalline grid structure around the Earth as lines of light in the atmosphere. Use the out breath to beam your heart love and well-being through this grid.

Charge and heal the Crystalline Earth Grid by shining *ahimsa* to all from your golden heart.

Prayer

May all beings be at peace. May all beings awake in Oneness.
I am at peace in Divine Oneness.

Chapter 11

Truth (*satya*)

The truth will set you free.
(John 8:32)

Truth is the foundation stone of the universe. Truth is who we are. Unequivocal. Some truths are only relative to the moment, ever changing and always in flux. These truths pertain to earthly life and the flow of change as ever present as the tide and the wind. These we have to learn to accept without judgement or falter, just as a tree which bends in the wind or flotsam bobbing in the tide. Know that we are always taken care of, for beyond relative truth there is an immutable universal truth in operation in God's universe. We are in touch with this Universal Truth while we sleep deeply or while meditating. When you awake refreshed to your core from sleep, you awake ready for another day fresh with a deep subconscious reminder of who you are and why you are here. Although for the ordinary person, this truth is unconscious, through meditation, we consciously awaken this truth within. Meditation, with deeper and deeper intensity and intent to know the truth will pay results and the beauty of it is, it is available to everyone for we carry that truth within us. We need go nowhere or attain a sometime-never perfect moment to start, just meditate now and it makes the moment perfect. In self-realisation, we *know* that we are God. All relative truths cease to matter because Universal Truth of all of creation is revealed to us. Each and every one of us can touch this precious store of inner, unchanging truth when we meditate with the intention to have this truth revealed. In prayer, we can fervently ask with the sure knowledge that we will be answered. Repeatedly demand: 'Father, reveal thyself.' Let loose all doubt, fear, barriers to truth or bar on love.

In bare-faced honesty, as aspirants on the homeward spiritual path, we must also speak the truth as is right. Ask yourself: Do I always speak the truth? Do my words flow as honey from my tongue? Sweet, with an honest intention to be compassionate? There are times when speaking your truth will be challenging. That is where discernment and tact come in. It is not always right to tell the whole truth if it will harm another physically, mentally, emotionally or spiritually. You will be challenged on the spiritual path to be increasingly vigilant and discerning of the right action to take moment by moment. That might be to stay quiet to save another's skin or to protect them from emotional pain and suffering. Be frankly honest with your motives: did I speak to hurt the other person? Did I speak from pride, seeking to look important? Was I seeking to dramatise bad news or carry malicious gossip?

As you advance on the spiritual path, you will also be challenged to hold your truth as a quiet, private store of truth between just you and God. You learn to refrain from telling all your garnered truths and spill them from your lips before those who would not respect Truth. Learn to listen to that inner voice of knowing about what is the right thing to do in each and every passing moment: to speak or not speak, to act or not act, that is the question. The Bible cautions us against revealing our innermost secret relationship with God.

Give not that which is holy to the dogs, neither cast you your pearls before swine, lest they trample them under their feet.
(Matthew 7:6)

Instead, learn to revere and hold as holy the truth within you. Speaking out of turn to those who are not in tune with this higher vibration would be to open to ridicule or, most importantly, disperse the very power and magnetism which you seek to contain during meditation. Some things are just between you and God, to be beheld in the glory of your inner being.

Tuning in with Universal Truth guides us in exactly the right word/silence, action/inaction to do in any moment. As a gauge, ask your inner sense of knowing before you act or speak – will my words or deeds, harm or heal? It is your intention behind the words or actions which is most important. This is when bare-faced truth with our motivations is needed. How much do I seek to heal? How much am I secretly wishing to harm? Living under Truth, we learn to harbour no false motivations which might seem fair on the surface but with a hidden intent to harm. Be honest with yourself. See it as a positive new revelation if you uncover a secret agenda, for your wish to bring all dissembling into the light of day, will befit you as a child of God to then let it go with each conscious breath, becoming lighter, purer and Truth personalised.

Sometimes, it is necessary to speak the truth even when you know it will harm another. Once all your hidden motivations are washed clear in the light of Spirit, your level of discernment increases. It is not our role to take on the pain of each person we meet who is suffering. Firstly, trust God's Law justly metes out suffering equal to all karma and for that soul to grow accordingly. Secondly, whatever that soul may be facing might be easy for you to do but know that sometimes you have to step back and let them grow, even if that means a level of suffering. Just as a child needs to grow into adulthood and learn to stand on his or her own two feet with all the challenges to life, so as a parent/friend figure, we can discern when it is right to help and when our help is actually hindering that soul from learning their own soul lessons. As we open to truth, we realise that sometimes we must let the other soul suffer in order to grow. To impede that process might be to incur more karma for ourselves or to encourage the soul to be dependent on external aid. It is the path of every soul to connect in our sacred heart of hearts with God and to live the truth of that in this incarnation.

Pranayama: Surya Bhedana (Piercing the Sun)

This is single nostril breathing with a specific focus of cleansing the *pingala nadi* which starts on the right side of the base (*muladhara*) chakra and passes the right nostril before ending on the right petal of the brow (ajna) chakra. *Surya* meaning 'Sun' is a warming energy. The left nostril and the *ida nadi* are associated with our body's cooling energy and linked to the moon. So, we will only be breathing in through the right nostril and breathing out of the left nostril.

Sit with the spine upright, chin level and make *mrigi mudra* (right hand poised over the face, so that the thumb can close the right nostril, ring and little fingers to close the left nostril, index and middle fingers tucked towards the palm).

Close your left nostril and inhale through your right, visualising the breath travelling down the psychic passage (*pingala*) to the base chakra.

Then close the right and exhale through the left, following the flow of breath up the left passage (*ida)* and out the left nostril. Continue in this manner, inhale right, exhale left, for 1 to 3 minutes.

Rose Temple of the Heart Meditation

Let the silence descend upon you from the stillness of the breath.

Be aware of breathing from the heart, each heart petal vibrating with the beauty of each breath.

Visualise a most beautiful garden, where every plant is lovingly tended. Each bloom is shining and offering its best. Walk with reverence, noting how each flower shines more beautifully than the last.

In the centre of the garden, you are drawn to the divine fragrance of a pale pink rose which shines with a pure effulgence of spirit. The fragrance draws you into the centre of the rose.

The light shines through the delicate pink petals forming a heavenly temple around you. You are bathed in the glorious light of unconditional love.

Let the vibration of love spiritualise and raise each chakra in turn.

Affirmation:

I am heavenly love and truth.

Chapter 12

Absence of Anger (*akrodha*)

'He was angry with me, he attacked me, he defeated me, he robbed me,' – those who dwell on such thoughts will never be free from hatred.

'He was angry with me, he attacked me, he defeated me, he robbed me,' – those who do not dwell on such thoughts will surely become free from hatred.

(From *The Dhammapada*, translated by Eknath Easwaran, founder of the Blue Mountain Center of Meditation, copyright 1985, 2007; reprinted by permission of Nilgiri Press, P. O. Box 256, Tomales, CA 94971, www.bmcm.org)

Just as a single raindrop cannot be experienced in a storm, so too, peace cannot be known in a maelstrom of anger. Once you can learn to face the internal irritations head on without flinching, you will have mastered the physical.

A deep insight into the human experience involves intense attention on remaining constant no matter what arises within. All is merely fluctuation due to latent tendencies, pre-natal or post-natal karma. You have to sit within the agitation, finding the eye of the storm. Find the calm centre and focus attention there as *prana* builds in intensity in that area of the body. Hold attention calmly. If you can maintain a detached intensity of focus, then the egg cracks open to reveal fresh insight. Do not allow ego to step in too intensely and get in the way of calmness nor too little, then the intensity of *prana* cannot build enough. Aim to reveal and crack open the 'locked' pockets of irritation by calmly holding intense focus with infinite patience. It may seem like a long time to wait if you are experiencing agitation, but know that in reality it only takes a few breaths of calmly intense focus for the shift to happen. This is when your mastery training of the senses, such as indifference to extreme heat or cold, or breath practices used in this book, will come into play. You will be learning to ride the irritation without focusing on it, instead focus on *what is behind it?* Keep praying *'God, reveal Thyself'*. God is hidden behind the irritation. Wouldn't it be wonderful to know God better in your heart? Have the spiritual stamina to stay the course in calmness.

In the same manner, intense emotion of guilt, blame, grief or hate 'locks in' our spirit through deeper chords of attachment to matter. Too little focus or too much focus is both extremes. Experiment with finding the happy medium between extremes. Look for the path of restraint from mental fluctuations. In order to transcend the human experience takes both intense focus and living within the expectation that in the very next moment, God will reveal Himself and all the mysteries of creation. Alchemy can be used positively or negatively. That is: to use intent, strong mental focus and emotion to will something to happen. Negative alchemy binds us even more to the wheel of birth and rebirth through ego-identification with more desire objects. Positive alchemy frees us from bondage to the human condition as we let go of the reins of control and pre-conceived expectation, we live a divine life in this one.

Cooling *Pranayama: Chandra Bhedana* (Piercing the Moon)

This is single nostril breathing with a specific focus of cleansing the *ida nadi* which starts on the left side of the base (*muladhara*) chakra and passes the left nostril before ending on the left petal of the brow (*ajna*) chakra. *Chandra* meaning 'moon' is a cooling energy. So we will only be breathing in through only the left nostril and breathing out through the right nostril.

Sit with the spine upright, chin level and make *mrigi mudra* (right hand poised over the face, so that the thumb can close the right nostril, ring and little fingers to close the left nostril, index and middle fingers tucked towards the palm).

Close your right nostril and inhale through your left, visualising the breath travelling down the psychic passage (*ida*) to the base chakra.

Then close the left and exhale through the right, following the flow of breath up the right passage (*pingala*) and out the right nostril. Continue in this manner, inhale left, exhale right, for 1 to 3 minutes.

Meditation on the Golden Light of Spirit

Bring your awareness to the tail bone and your connection into the golden heart of the Earth. Let the golden light flow up the spine, illuminating each chakra in turn.

Open the fontanel on the crown and connect with the highest vibration star above your head. Aim higher than you have ever connected before.

Allow your consciousness to be bathed in pure white starlight.

Let all heaviness and the earthly plane fall away.

Your heart opens to receive more light with each breath.

You are blessed with the Golden Light of Spirit, washed clean and clear, inside and out.

Prayer

Divine Father, bless me with the light of the Holy Spirit.

Chapter 13

Renunciation (*tyaga*)

The mind absorbed in the Divine even while engaging in earthly activities gets purified. Purifying your mind means that your sense of doership vanishes and God becomes the doer.
(Jack Hawley, *The Bhagavad Gita: A Walkthrough for Westerners,* 5:7)

Renunciation is relinquishing the ego claim for ownership of the body, possessions, the actions we do or the fruit of those actions. Renunciation is the true spiritual path that allows us to finally slough off being bound to continual birth and rebirth on the karmic wheel and suffering incarnation in a physical body again and again.

All actions focused through the little ego-self incur karma. Even *sattvic* actions which are done for the benefit of others incur karma, albeit a lesser karma than selfish activity from an active *rajistic* or ignorant *tamasic* motivation (see chapter 6 on the three *gunas*). Through renunciation, we finally learn how to free ourselves from the little ego will, handing over agency to God's Will.

The wonder of karma yoga is learning to loosen those cords of attachment to each action, such as 'it is I who walks the dog', and to a vested interest in the result of the action. Deeper states of meditation reveal veil after veil shrouding God's light at our core. We realise that this body is a convenient vehicle to move around in a physical realm and that this body is a gift. We do not own it. It is a parcel of light to house our soul while in this world which is not our abode. Ego thinks it is the body and deludes us time and time again to falsely seeing the world through two external eyes and the five senses. By buying into attachment to the feedback from the senses, we remain as one asleep to the truth that this world is God's dream world. Practising sense withdrawl (*pratyahara*) by pulling our *prana* flow back from the four limbs, each one of the senses and even the spine to the spiritual eye (*ajna*), is vital in learning how to withdraw consciousness from the allure of *maya* (illusion).

In handing over agency for actions, we acknowledge God as the true doer behind the cosmic illusion of *maya*, us and any physical action. In the example of walking the dog: God is the dog, we are God and even the action of walking is God. There is only Cosmic Consciousness or God.

Hand over the outcome of any action, since it is not us who act, the fruit of the action is irrelevant. Trust that God's divine planning is in operation through our small part, God acts through us. Therefore we cannot fail. Chapter five of the Gita details how to obtain soul freedom through inner renunciation.

As the lotus floating on the surface of muddy water stays untouched by the water, when you offer all actions to the Divine and surrender any yearning for the results, you cannot be tainted.
(Jack Hawley, *The Bhagavad Gita: A Walkthrough for Westerners*, 5:10)

What if you were to live each moment as if the Lord's glory did shine in and all around you and through you at all times?

What if, you acknowledged that God is witnessing all your actions? What if, you found that it was not you who was the agent in your actions, but God? How would that change how you approach each small gesture or grand performance? Could you imagine that there was no one else present in your daily actions and interactions but you and God? That each moment is a sacred communion with God.

Perhaps we can realise that in any action, we work from a desire or need for a particular outcome. Take a moment to reflect on what you have already done today, before reading this book. How many times were you mindful that God was witnessing these actions through your eyes? In other words, how many times were you acting *consciously* as a courageous soul having a human experience? It is easy to get caught up in the hum drum monotony of living or to be so driven by time constraints and duty that we act unconsciously. And so another day may come to a close which has been full of selfishly driven needs and desires. Many of those actions may have been duty-bound, but acting consciously takes living to a whole new level of being. We learn to *use* the mundane and duty-bound actions and to transmute them into divinely-led actions by remembering God in them. Act as if God were acting through your hands, your voice and your presence and so doing participate in your worldly role as an ambassador of God.

We will take a break here to reflect on what it means to be acting consciously and with God-focus.

How many times today did I remember consciously that I am a spiritual being having a human experience?

How did I express myself in that moment? From love? Or by looking for Divine approval? Or by looking for approval or praise from my fellow human beings? Who was the 'self' that was being expressed: little ego-self or Expansive God-Self?

Perhaps here is the time to acknowledge attachment to the reward or result of my actions. Do I seek approval and what nature of reward motivates me? How long has this been the pattern for me? Does it stem from childhood or adolescence?

Acknowledging and bringing into the light of discernment, all selfish motivations which hitherto drove us to act in response to certain stimuli and circumstances can be very healing. A cup which is full to over-flowing is very difficult to fill with a new way of being. It is healthy to relinquish a hold on what drives us selfishly in order to move into a higher vibrational way of being: that of handing over our actions to act as if God were acting through us. That is the true meaning of renunciation. Those of you who are still locked into the old order of third-dimensional thinking may find this concept difficult to get your head around at first. So I'll make it simple. Do you find happiness in the mundane tasks of daily living? Or do you find them boring? Boredom is a sign that how you are operating your life isn't divinely satisfying or fulfilling. Feeling bored is a signpost on the spiritual highway that something is lacking in your life. I'm sure that if you are reading this book you have already realised that transient material acquisitions or the next holiday aren't going to be fulfilling and satisfying to your soul. I know that you have a hunger in your soul to be back in Unity and Oneness with God and are actively soul-searching to find how you might achieve that while in this incarnation.

Well, I'll let you know the secret: it's in the small, seemingly mundane tasks that you can change how you operate in this world. Externally, you will still be acting as before: cleaning, working, dealing with the people in your life and fulfilling your role but in the secret inner relationship that you are building with God, you will find huge changes. You will no longer be acting from an ego-driven desire or perceived need but because you have given your life to God to work great works through your small human vessel. Make no mistake, this is the greatest single change that you could make in how you direct the ship of your life, to chart it into the hands of God, the master captain, who can safely guide you through all known charted waters and those that have yet to be charted. Here are some of the wonders which having God as your master oarsman are in store for you:

- Renewed vigour and zest for living
- Release of anxiety and stress (God quickly affirms for us that we will be alright, even when intellectually you do not hold all the answers, you will just know with a constancy of faith, that you will be OK)

- A sense of direction and purpose
- Freedom (and here's one of the divine paradoxes: it is by handing over our lives to our divine master, God, that freedom is found. It was a naivety of our perception to believe that separateness was a reality and that personal autonomy in itself gave us freedom. Selfish actions only result in bondage to the karmically just and exact wheel of birth and rebirth)
- A deepening of your inner relationship with God and a certainty of knowledge that you are not alone, have never been abandoned and will never be separate from God, no matter what you do, think or say (although you will unsurprisingly have a closer relationship when you are no longer riddled with guilt born from a realisation that you have acted selfishly or harmfully towards others at any time)

The exercise we will work on for this chapter is to release preconceived expectations to results of our actions which keep us bound to both the resulting outcome and to self-judgement that it didn't go exactly as we planned.

Prayer

Divine Father, illuminate me. Lead me from ignorance into knowledge. Reveal Thyself as the sole doer of all my actions.

Handing over the Breath

Sitting upright with the hands and eyes at rest, inhale softly to the count of 12, hold the breath for 12 and release the breath for a count of 12. Repeat for several breaths, with a mental chant of OM with the focus on the brow chakra on the retention of the breath.

Let the breath return to a gentle inhale, a mental chant of OM in retention and a steady exhale, staying with the flow of the breath.

Ask yourself: Is it I who breathes? Notice any attachment to physical sensation.

Ask within: Does God breathe this body? Notice that God is continually breathing *prana* into this physical body through the medulla oblongata at the back of the head.

Even as you breathe in, hand ownership of the breath back to God.

Offer each exhale as a blessing or gift to God.

Active Meditation

Choose a short mundane task with which to practise renunciation to God, such as washing a cup, sweeping the floor or cleaning the toilet. Decide for the next minute or two to remain conscious that God acts through you: God is the object, the action and the actor.

Keep your mind focused on God breathing through your medulla oblongata (back of the skull) and that God operates these hands.

Quietly in the background of your mind, chant 'OM, God'.

Observe God looking out from the eyes and moving the hands.

In your heart, offer all attachment to the outcome of the action: you are solely observing God operating through this physical body. Offer any cords of expectation of the end result as a gift to God.

Affirmation

I am Light, God is Light. I am God. God and I are One.

Chapter 14

Peace (*shanti*)

Open the door of your calmness and let the footsteps of silence gently enter the temple of all your activities. Perform all duties serenely, saturated with peace. Behind the throb of your heart, you shall feel the throb of God's peace.
(Paramahansa Yogananada, *Inner Peace: How to be Calmly Active and Actively Calm*)

Peace is our natural God-like state. The opposite of peace is nervous energy. One sends out the sweetest fragrance like a balm, bringing an aura of serenity. The other brings agitation, exactly like the jagged lines around a drawing in a child's comic which is palpable to all they meet. The myriad of distractions which modern life presents constantly lures us from inner sanctity and peace into agitated frenzy. As yogis, we learn to still the waters of the soul into calmness, unruffled by transient change visiting the narrative of our life. Change is inevitable. We can learn to regard each passing change with just as much consequence as the shadow of a storm cloud on the water. Let nothing ruffle your inner peace: treat pleasant or unpleasant circumstances with the same calm indifference. Indifference does not mean that you do not have compassion. On the contrary, spiritual strength is found in being actively calm, to face each challenge with a will to be as constant as the tide.

The key to retaining inner peace is to meditate on peace; let this peace become deeper and more profound each time you meditate so that peace becomes a palpable presence in your life. This is God.

Know that changes in this physical world do not affect your

soul or God-like self, which is only ever at peace, untouched by worldly events. Therefore the next time you feel agitation or restlessness, recall that this is not God-like. This is not who you really are. Once consciously recognised, you have the opportunity to change mentally by releasing agitation, like discharging static electricity into the ground.

Meditation builds a magnetic strength of inner peace until you can walk through crowds of agitated people and remain calm. Peace does not mean passiveness. It is a strong and resilient depth which arises from our inner core, from God. Day by day, in a consistent meditation practice that magnetic depth of peace and bliss deepens: this is how we can know God.

And the peace of God that surpasses all understanding will guard your hearts and minds in Christ Jesus.
(Philippians 4:7)

Prayer of Saint Francis

Lord, make me an instrument of Thy peace,
Where there is hatred, let me sow love;
Where there is injury, pardon;
Where there is doubt, faith;
Where there is despair, hope;
Where there is darkness, light;
Where there is sadness, joy.

World peace may appear to be absent in the physical world as conflicts perpetuate between nations and religions. However, when any calamitous event, like the Twin Towers falling, sends reverberations around the world, people's heartfelt urge is to help one another. Race, nationality or religion is irrelevant. We only see our brother or sister in need of aid. Choose to actively *be* peace by praying for peace every day.

Peace is always present but it is sometimes hidden. Peace is our true nature as a child of God. If we are not at peace within, then there can be no peace in our lives. It is each of us who cumulatively matter in bringing world peace for it is a heaven we carry in our hearts: we, each of us, create peace as collective reality on earth. So the next time you find the undercurrents of unrest in the waters of your soul, remember that you matter to us all. Stop. Breathe 'stillness' upon the waters within.

Peace comes from within. Do not seek it without.
(Gautama Buddha)

Prithvi (Earth) *Pranayama*

Become aware of your breath in the abdomen: a steady inhale inflates the belly and relaxes on the out-breath.

Fill the abdomen with 'Peace' as you breathe in. *Be* 'Peace' as you breathe out.

Become aware of *muladhara* (base) chakra. Let your roots flow down to the golden heart of Mother Earth, your soul light co-mingling with the golden light of the Earth.

Become One light.

Let that light flow back up your roots, through the spine, out through *sahasrara* (crown) chakra to connect with the highest light above you.

Bring your consciousness back into the middle of the head, gazing softly and steadily towards the centre of Christ Consciousness (brow) chakra.

Become aware of your breath.

Visualise your spine as a hollow tube, connected into the golden heart of Mother Earth.

As you breathe in, She breathes in.

As you breathe out, She breathes out.

Become as a pore on the surface of the Earth.

As She breathes in, She breathes through you.

As She breathes out, She breathes out through you.
Come into synchronicity with the breath of the Earth.
Verbally chant 'OM' as the Earth breathes out, 12 times.
Mentally chant 'OM' as the Earth breathes out, 12 times.
Let go into the cosmic breathing of the Earth: You and She are One. She lives to serve peace. You live to serve peace.

Meditation: *Be* the Peace you want to see in the world

Meditate on the resonance of the meaning of 'peace' or '*shanti*'.

Imagine that the word 'peace' or '*shanti*' is gently dropped into your core as a grace from God.

Let that hand of grace reveal peace at your inner core.

'Prayer, Father reveal thy Peace'.

If the mind wanders, mentally chant: *Shanti, shanti, shanti* or Peace, peace, peace.

Patience and Love reveals peace.

Love God with all your heart and soul. Love more intensely than you have ever loved before.

Let Peace be revealed as a strong presence: this is God.

Shanti Path Peace Prayer

Om Dyau, Shanti Rantariksha Gwam,
Shanti Prithvi, Shanti Rapah,
Shanti Roshadhayah, Shanti Vanas Patayah,
Shanti Vishwed Devah, Shanti Brahma,
Shanti Sarvag Wam,
Shanti Shanti Reva, Shanti Sa Ma, Shanti Redhi,
Om Shanti Shanti Shanti.

Meaning:

Unto the Heaven be Peace, Unto the Sky and the Earth be

Peace,
Peace be unto the Water, Unto the Herbs and Trees be Peace,
Unto all the Gods be Peace, Unto Brahma and unto All be
Peace.
And may we realise that Peace.
Om Peace Peace Peace.

NB: The beautiful song of the Shanti Path Peace prayer can be
heard online at www.living-lightly.co.uk and Youtube.

Chapter 15

Absence of Fault-Finding (*apaishunam*)

If you want peace of mind, do not find fault with others. Rather learn to see your own faults. Learn to make the whole world your own. No-one is a stranger, my child; the whole world is your own.
(Sri Sarada Devi)

Time here on earth is limited. How best do we wish to remember this incarnation: as someone who frittered precious time looking outwards, caught up in *maya's* (illusion) of the narrative of this incarnation or someone who woke up to soul reality as cosmic consciousness through looking inwards? Changing a habit of a lifetime can be difficult. Once you turn your attention to if and how you have been judging others, you may find that it has been a full-time occupation, sitting safely behind the screen of the TV, social media or the steering wheel of the car. Just because the object of your sharp derision cannot hear the judgement that you meted out, does not mean that it hasn't fallen home, even if you didn't actually intend to harm them. We are under the misguided notion that it's harmless to back-bite or run others down in secret. When you tune into your own aura, you'll find that every seed of judgement of others has become lodged there as a sour note.

When listening to someone sharing their heartfelt woes, how quick are you to issue summary judgement? We have usually made a snap decision on how to react to the person before they have even finished speaking. Being really listened to is a very healing experience. Tips on how to listen: place the speaker in a healing column of light, bless him or her to speak from their highest place as a soul, bring your breathing to a non-reactive quietness, quashing any judgement, just let the person say what's on their heart, concentrating on sending love from your soul. Reserve your reply until they have finished speaking. Tune into your soul's inner voice in response, then speak.

Learning to respond from a soul perspective is to be truly *sattvic* (benevolent). When you accept that it's OK to have very different viewpoints, it allows for a commonality and solution to come to the fore. Seen from a cosmic perspective, each soul is part of the same whole. It only takes one soul to wake up and speak, not to the small ego in anguish, but to the perfect soul that can be seen, beneath the pain, in the other's eyes. Have the courage to speak heart to heart to the God within each person you meet.

Don't judge a man until you've walked a mile in his shoes.
Traditional

How can we possibly know all the motivations a person had in order to present themselves to the world? Courtroom judges take all extenuating circumstances into consideration. We can make snap judgements just by reading someone's body language, even as we get very good at it! Can you halt the judgement and step back inwards from the world arena into the language of the soul, where we are One?

The Law of Attraction reflects every thought, word or deed back to us. Every harsh judgement sent as an axe, needle or barb of others, comes back to undermine your self-esteem, beneath your own skin.

The mental suffering you create is always some form of non-acceptance, some form of unconscious resistance to what is.
On the level of thought, the resistance is some form of judgement.
The intensity of the suffering depends on the degree of resistance to the present moment.
(From the book The Power of Now. Copyright © 2004 by

Eckhart Tolle. Reprinted with permission of New World Library, Novato, CA. www.newworldlibrary.com)

So question within: where am I harbouring resistance to releasing judgement?

It is better to turn our vast resources into a full-time commitment to bettering ourselves instead of picking faults with others. All disagreements stem from seeing others as separate. Duality sees separation. Unity allows for many perspectives being correct, even if differing. Do you remember the story of the seven blind men who were asked to describe the elephant? One man felt the trunk and said it was long and snake-like. Another felt the leg and said it was as wide as a tree, and so on. Each had a different description of the elephant and yet all of them were correct. God knows that the visible physical world is just part of the Unity of all that it is. Our path is to look beyond the surface to perceive God as omnipresent.

Chanting A-U-M

In this physical world, having the illusion of duality, there is a constant flux of the three stages of creation for all life-forms: creation, sustaining and then ebbing into dissolution; incarnating, physical life being sustained and then physical death; the in-breath, breath retention and then out-breath. The extended sound of OM represents these three stages as A-U-M. AUM is the conglomerate sound of the creative, preservative and dissolving vibrations in Nature.

A – Akara: the creative principle
U – Ukara: the sustaining principle
M – Makara: the dissolving principle

AUM is the creator of all things, manifesting as cosmic light and cosmic sound. Chanting AUM lets us forget the restrictions of the human body and feel the AUM vibrating into a deeper perception of our cosmic body. We can feel our consciousness vibrating everywhere with the ever-expanding astral sound of AUM.

An advanced yogi can hear the sound of AUM in his body and can see its light in his spiritual eye.
(Paramahansa Yogananda, *God Talks with Arjuna: The Bhagavad Gita*, p.1008)

Chant A-U-M aloud for at least 12 breaths until the resonance of the three, sound as One.

Breathe in, mentally chanting Aaa. Hold the retention of the inhale, mentally chanting Uuu. Breathe out, mentally chanting Mmmm.

Listen to the reverberations of AUM. Focus on letting go, in acceptance of all that is.

Visuddhi (throat) Chakra Meditation – Listening with Detachment

Let the breath become calm and quiet. Focus on the soft sound of the breath in the throat and the back of the palate.

Take your awareness to sounds outside of the room.

Try to let the sounds pass through unhindered by labels 'that's a car, my neighbour, the postman, birdsong, etc.'.

Listen to the sounds as if you were a newborn: they are just sounds.

Concentrate on the quiet space within, behind those sounds.

Sounds simply pass uninterrupted by a reflex thought-response.

Let listening be a quiet inner experience.

Realise that there is a hair's breadth moment where you have a choice, to respond to the mind's gathering of a thought, or simply to let it pass.

Let the inner listening space become larger and quieter.

The space becomes so profound that random thoughts do not intrude.

Be in this inner quiet, listening to the white silence ...

Prayer

Divine Father, let my listening be so intense, that I hear the sound of your softly returning footsteps in my heart.

Chapter 16

Compassion (*daya*)

'Love the Lord your God with all your **heart** and with all your soul and with all your strength and with all your mind', and, 'Love your neighbour as yourself.'
(Luke 10:27)

A sign of your deepening inner alignment is an increasing sensitivity to feeling another's suffering. At times, this heightened awareness can be painful and hard to bear. Compassion towards all beings is being able to feel what other's feel, warts and all, and to still respond positively and lovingly. Compassion helps us remain centred and calm, even in the face of extreme suffering, for compassion links us to the highest quality of unconditional love. We become the feminine aspect of God: the Divine Mother. Is not God herself always extending the greatest of Compassions? We are continually offered an overflowing of Divine Mercy to forego our old harmful patterns of being. Compassion is the bridge with which we realise that those who harmed you erred because they were as children. The Divine Mother still loves all her naughty children, even if they have been steeped in wrong-doing life after life. Emulating the Divine Mother and extending compassion, not retaliation to those who may have wronged you is a mark of your spiritual progress and awakening.

We cannot continue as human beings to see each other as flawed or 'bad' or unforgiveable if we place them in the light of the Divine feminine principle. Shift your awareness and, although the deeds have not changed, we can perceive them as being acted through the pain and suffering of another who thinks: 'I am in pain so I make others suffer.' When we shift our consciousness to a higher principle, we tap into a deeper wisdom which knows that whatever we give, we also receive.

Sitting within Compassion lets you witness suffering and respond by being more loving, not less. It is a conscious choice. Compassion has a way of transforming on several levels. Imagine you were a stray dog which had only ever experienced poor treatment at the hands of humans, you might respond aggressively to a Good Samaritan at first, but with kindness, your behaviour would start to change. Acceptance and compassion can change even the most taciturn person.

Try experimenting: decide to be friendly towards a neighbour or colleague who is always grumbling negatively and isn't well liked. The likelihood is that people will avoid him or her. What if you choose to act differently? Could you spend time to talk with them as if you were really pleased to see them? Or do small thoughtful acts of kindness, like run small errands, take out their rubbish, share food or a small gift? People rarely stay grumpy once they no longer feel estranged. Perhaps you could offer a bridge of compassion to help them shift into a happier response? Do not under estimate the power of love and small acts of kindness. Just think of any times when you were grumpy, were you secretly trying to elicit attention and a favourable response but like a toddler, you just were not adept at seeking the most appropriate way of receiving loving attention? Imagine or remember times when you were not so spiritually aware. How many times did you react poorly before you realised that there was a better way? Who or what helped you to change your approach? Perhaps you can be the catalyst to help a lost soul at just the pivotal time?

Compassion can move mountains. It is a soothing salve on a wounded spirit. Compassion seeks to make no judgement except to extend the loving hand of friendship.

In this exercise, we will be linking with the Divine Mother. The Divine Mother is the perfect epitome of motherly love. For many of us, at times our earthly mother loved conditionally: 'Be a good or quiet child and mother will present you with love and affection' but these were withdrawn when you were seen to be 'bad'. The Divine Mother fills us with love unconditionally no matter how many times we slip up or fall. Through unconditional love, we can learn to love our emotional wounds and nurse them back to health in the knowledge that our soul was always perfect and whole.

Pranayama: Cutting the inhale (*Viloma Pranayama*)

In this version of *viloma pranayama*, the inhale is interrupted in the form of pauses: inhale, pause, inhale, pause, inhale, pause, inhale, pause. Then a long exhale. The pauses between the breaths offer us a respite from the physical motion of the breath and an opportunity to expand into stillness. Stepping or cutting the inhale allows us to deepen our connection with the pauses between breaths. Physiologically, it helps us to extend the inhale. The aim is to have the exhale smooth and long. Both the inhale and exhale should be quiet and softly executed.

Inhale (cutting the breath)   Long,smooth exhale

Complete 12 breaths.

Meditation on the Divine Mother

Sit quietly observing the breath as it becomes softer and settles.

Imagine sitting on a large square base, like the solid stone base of a pyramid.

In the centre of the square imagine a golden shaft of light connecting down into the earth. Draw that golden light up through the spine, igniting each chakra in turn until you reach the heart. Allow golden light to circulate around the heart chamber.

Connect with the golden light in the spine as you draw gold

light through the head to connect with a fine white gold light above your head. Imagine being showered in golden light, washing you clear to the four points of the square base. Feel or imagine the solidity of the square base. Ask yourself: what do I have to release? Energetically hand it over to the golden stream of light to be bathed away.

Take your awareness to the Unconditional Love Chakra which sits above the heart chakra and beneath the throat chakra.

Prayer

Divine Mother, please be with me. Place me in your compassion and divine love. Teach me to love with the depth of your love for all beings.

Breathe in Compassion and breathe out golden light.

Practise for at least 12 breaths.

Ask yourself: what do I have to let go of?

Breathe in compassion and hand it over to the golden light.

Ask yourself: what harm have I ever done in thought, word or deed?

Breathe in Compassion and transmute into golden light on the exhale.

Ask: what do I have to forgive?

Breathe in Compassion and transmute into gold light on the exhale.

Practise *Viloma Pranayama* for 12 breaths. Breathe in Compassion on each step of the inhale and golden light on the exhale.

Return the breath to a long, soft inhale and exhale with a pause between the breath (internal retention). With consciousness in the Unconditional Love chakra, use the mental mantra 'I am Compassion' on the pause.

Appeal to the Divine Mother: '*Divine Mother express your*

compassion through me. Guide me to be more compassionate in my life.'

Release the focus on the breath. Notice the soft, compassionate quality of the inhale and exhale from the Unconditional Love chakra.

Imagine an infinity symbol being traced in burning white light within the chakra. Consciously trace this figure of 8 in your mind until you can feel the bright light within the chakra.

Sit within the quiet, gazing calmly towards the brow chakra for as long as you can.

Prayer

Divine Mother, express your compassion through me. Guide me to be more compassionate in my life.

Chapter 17

Absence of Greed (*aloluptvam*)

Hell has three gates which lead to the destruction of the soul's
welfare: lust, anger and greed. These three, man should abandon.
(Bhagavad Gita 16:21)

Metaphysically, the gates which Gita refers to are the three lower
chakras, when man allows himself to gravitate to these lower
tamasic modes of being, he finds himself caught in entrenched
selfish habits. In seeking body-identified pleasure, he instead
finds himself trapped in a web of matter and pain. Greed is a
negative force associated with the attraction and repulsion at the
manipura (navel) chakra. How many times do we take more than
we need? Greed always comes from a fear of lack.

In this chapter, we will be focusing on the seemingly deep-
seated desire to be sated with food when the real need placed
within every soul is be filled by the Holy Spirit of the cosmic
fire of God. We will learn how physical food can never suffice
to fill that void. There is inbuilt in every soul the longing to be
back in Oneness. That yearning of the soul, in being housed
in physical body, has been mapped out during infancy into
the physical environment in the mistaken belief that physical
sustenance can make us whole. However, like everything else
in the physical realm, all is transient. At most, the physical body
is only sustained for a few hours before it 'hungers' again for
food. To be unconsciously caught within the cycle of constantly
eating to fill an insatiable need, is to be snared by *maya* (cosmic
illusion). But there is another way.

In the developed world there are very few people who wake
up each morning with nothing to eat. I dare say there may have
been times in your life when money was tight, but still most of

us have never known true hunger. Greed comes from a fear of hunger or from pure indulgence of the senses in league with each other. Chefs say that the eyes eat the dish before the belly and that we feast on the sight of food first. So, here is our first line of stepping back from being engrossed in the cycle of greed. Think about that moment when food is placed in front of you. There are all the body's physical reactions: mouth salivates, smell wafts up, belly starts to churn in anticipation ... in that moment before you dive in, fork wielding, catch yourself. Leave the cutlery where it is.

Ask yourself: is this food going to fill me emotionally or spiritually?

Prayer spiritualises the food in front of you. It raises the *prana* (life force) level within the atoms so that you can be filled for what you really hunger for: spiritual sustenance. You will also find that you need less food. The only reason that we eat food is to be nourished with cosmic *prana*, which we receive directly through the medulla oblongata at the back of the head and indirectly from the air we breathe, sunlight, water and food. That cosmic *prana* is the building block of God's creative fire throughout the whole of creation. When we pray, we become mindful that cosmic *prana* is the food itself, inherent in its creation and in our own physical bodies. This is our link back home to Oneness. In prayer we remember that. We leave behind mechanical consumption of food for a life of consciously living in gratitude for all that has been provided for us. The Lord's Prayer or a blessing of your own devising will help you to ride beyond mindless eating. The most important thing is to become conscious. Empty, mind-elsewhere words are not a prayer. Remember that it is God who is in everything in creation, including the food, and be mindful and grateful for that.

Heavenly Father, Receive this food: make it holy. Let no impurity of greed defile it. Thy food comes from Thee, it is for Thy temple.

Spiritualise it. Spirit to Spirit goes. We are the petals of Thy manifestation; but Thou art the flower, It's life, beauty and loveliness. Permeate our souls with the fragrance of thy Presence.
(From *Whispers from Eternity* by Paramahansa Yogananda, 2008, Crystal Clarity Publishers, Nevada City, California)

We will explore different methods of filling up with spiritual *prana* but firstly, we will start with the process of physically eating. I invite you here to take a small snack such as a few nuts, a biscuit or a piece of fruit. These will be the subject of our meditation using focus on the senses to dive deeply into finding what is behind the senses. For this meditation, we will be using all five senses in concert as the inroad into a deeper awareness behind the physical identification and to free up entrapment within the cosmic illusion (*maya*): eyes devouring the sight, smelling intoxicating food aromas, taste explosions on the tongue, feeling texture and juice in the mouth and stomach, even deeply listening to the sound of the mastication. In this meditation, you may notice that this orchestra of the senses works in tandem but we can take this symphony as one and consciously recall that God is behind the experience as a whole.

Eating Meditation
Hold the food in your hand and let your eyes drink it in: colour, shape, light. Try to hold the mind in check from jumping to anticipate the act of eating.

Pray or bless your food. Visualise it in a column of light from its conception as a seed, through production, handling or preparation to the present moment in your hand.

Thank God for being in every part of that process.

Realise that God is contained in the food.

Close your eyes and take a small bite. Have awareness of the explosion of senses.

Chew slowly with lots of pauses to realise God is within this golden morsel of sunlight on your tongue.

Realise that God is within your very tongue.

Bless God through the food on your tongue.

Travel through the senses to reveal God behind them. Pray: *Father, Reveal thyself.*

You may realise the spiritualisation of the senses as a golden liquid on the tongue.

Be in the moment with the mind interiorised on God.

Swallow as if you have been offered the highest blessing of Divine Spirit.

Experience how that Holy Spirit light sits in the stomach as a fullness.

Realise it's not in the quantity of food but it is with the quality of holy *prana* blessing that we are filled.

When I was a small child, it was instinctual to be wholly present in the food I was eating. My blessing was to hum aloud as I chewed to raise the vibration of food while eating. Then, eating was a whole new depth of wonder with every mouthful. When asked why I did it, I recall saying it made the food taste better. (I must have been a strange child!) As an adult, I realise that every time I respond to delicious food by saying 'mmm', I am spiritualising my food with the cosmic sound AUM. I invite you to try humming 'mmm', with your focus on God as you eat. It's a wonderful experience of immersion in God!

Eating sparingly is good for spiritual advancement. Not just because it is good to learn to restrict the body's instinct for greed as a spiritual strength but because the body becomes sluggish if it is filled with too much food. The digestive fire dampens spiritual consciousness. The cosmic current is diverted from upward focus in the upper spinal centres to the stomach. If you have ever meditated after eating a largish meal, you will know what I mean. It's a constant fight against torpor as you have given the physical body a prior role of digestion. This then is a good indicator of why we eat in little amounts: firstly, as experienced in the Eating Meditation, when we spiritualise the food, we need less, and secondly, the digestive system isn't overloaded and overworked for hours. The gross process of digestion takes a huge effort from the physical body. Smaller amounts of light foods are easier for it to cope with and it can digest more efficiently.

Regarding dietary practices, know that there are subtle elements in food that significantly influence the mind and therefore shape mental attitudes. This creates a cycle similar to the situation with one's faith: you are what you eat, and you eat based on what you are ... sooner or later all serious spiritual aspirants have to face up to the issue of what they consume.
(Jack Hawley, *The Bhagavad Gita: A Walkthrough for Westerners*, 17:8)

There are certain types of food which the Bhagavad Gita states are easier for the body to digest. *Sattvic* foods are mainly vegan: fresh fruit and vegetables, raw or lightly cooked; whole grains; dairy milk* (nut milks); pulses; nuts and seeds; vegetable oils and natural sugars from dried fruit and honey#. *Rajistic* foods are spicy, hot, bitter or salty, including fish, fowl, lamb and eggs. *Tamasic* foods are stale, tasteless and lifeless, including any flesh of a higher mammal, as these are chemically and vibrationally injurious to spiritual well-being.

(Footnote: *Ethically sourced from a dairy herd where the calves are not taken from their mothers at two days old. #Ethically sourced honey from a local apiarist who can vouch for the welfare of the bees.)

It is very beneficial for the physical body to have regular abstinence from the process of eating, unless your doctor cautions against it. Fasting is restful for the physical body and allows the digestive system to recover from overwork. Fasts are also wonderful ways of linking more deeply with your spiritual practice by using the time to become quiet and meditate more deeply on God. If you have a particular concern, fast and meditate on it. I assure you that it will be most illuminating.

A fast can be of long (3 days), medium (1 day) or short term duration (breaking your fast late afternoon or evening). Drink plenty of water or herbal teas to flush toxins from your system and to allow the belly to feel 'full'.

While preparing and cooking food, prepare it consciously in the spirit of a spiritual blessing on the ingredients and the recipients of the food. Before starting the preparation, dedicate your hands and heart in prayer acknowledging God's light inherent in the food, your bodies, the action of preparing food, your mind and spirit and in all things. Feeding others with even a simple soup made truly from the heart laced with God's blessing is a truly spiritual experience for the giver and the receiver. You can learn to fill their spirit not just their stomachs.

Many saints and masters have thus learned to go long periods of time, even years, being totally nourished directly from the divine sustenance of *prana* or life force. The only reason that we eat at all is to distil the condensed *prana* of sunlight, soil and water from the food. This is a highly inefficient system which is wrought by the body only after a huge effort of digestion. This effort is what eventually tires and ages the whole system. Even a short fast can alleviate and reverse the ageing process inherent in the digestion of physical food.

Spiritual sustenance, on the other hand, links us directly with God, as the source of spiritual sunlight. *Yajna* is a specific fire ritual of making a spiritual offering of clarified butter (ghee) onto a fire to symbolise the food about to be consumed. While God as the cosmic spirit has no requirement for physical consumption, the ritual, however, places the devotee in a highly receptive state to be filled with spiritual *prana* and the liquid fire of divinely intoxicating nectar within the mouth, called *amrita*.

We can learn to provide our bodies with holy sustenance

of *amrita* by using a tongue *mudra* (a physical posture that completes a *nadi* energy circuit within the astral body). *Khechari mudra* is associated with *amrita*, the nectar or elixir of life which is secreted from *bindu*, a point situated at the posterior fontanel, and then collected at *vishuddhi* (throat) chakra. Perfection of this practice enables the yogi to trap the descending drops of *amrita* at *vishuddhi*, overcoming hunger and thirst, and rejuvenating the entire body.

Kshestra mudra is achieved by placing the tongue in a groove at the back of the soft palate in the mouth.

Meditation using Kshestra Mudra

Become still by taking awareness into the legs, knees, ankles, feet and toes and think: 'Be Still'. Withdraw awareness from the legs.

Take awareness into the arms, elbows, wrists, hands and fingers. Think: 'Be Still'. Withdraw awareness from the arms.

Take awareness into the belly. Think: 'Be Still'. Withdraw awareness to the chest.

Take awareness into the chest. Think: 'Be Still'. Withdraw awareness into the head.

Take awareness to focus smoothly and calmly on the brow.

Breathe from the brow using *Viloma Pranayama* (cutting the breath on the inhale only) for 12 breaths.

Place the tongue on the soft palate on the roof of the mouth. Focus on the tongue while maintaining a calm, even-focused breath.

You may experience a tingling, warmth, or electrical sensation in the tongue. Focus on receiving a flow of divine nectar (*amrita*) on or into the tongue itself. However you experience this *mudra*, maintain focus, with an expectancy of deepening the practice moment by moment.

Retain the breath after the inhale and build the intensity of focus on the tongue.

Allow each exhale to be long and smooth as if savouring a delicious taste.

Does the poignancy deepen with a pause after the exhale?

Maintain the *mudra* for as long as comfortable.

Focus on a feeling of bliss or sustenance. Gaze calmly and smoothly at the spiritual eye.

Lord's Prayer focusing on '*Give us our daily bread*'

Divine Father, who art in Heaven, hallowed be Thy name.
Thy kingdom come, Thy will be done on earth as it is in heaven.
Give us our daily bread *and forgive us our debts as we forgive*
our debtors,
And lead us not into temptation but deliver us from evil,
For Thine is the Kingdom, the Power and the Glory,
Forever and ever, Amen.

Chapter 18

Gentleness (*mardavam*)

In a gentle way, you can shake the world.
(Gandhi)

Gentleness is a stream of consciousness imbued with spiritual patience and harmony. God, as our divine parent, is ever gentle. No matter what we might do or how we might ignore Him, God is unoffended and holds no judgement. This then is our precedent for living through gentleness. We embody gentleness when, through meditation, we attune to a higher vibration of consciousness. In spiritual consciousness, we can only think, speak and act from a place of gentleness.

I'd like to share the understanding of gentleness which has been expressed by spiritual masters. Kabir, a fifteenth-century Indian mystic, describes ever finer states of God-consciousness being attained by refining and cleansing the 'fibres' of one's body, mind and soul to be increasingly more receptive to God. He equates the process of refinement though the metaphor of a loom. Ever increasing soul gentleness is the result of the process of spiritual refinement.

I weave your name on the loom of my mind,
To make my garment when you come to me.
My loom has ten thousand threads
To make my garment when you come to me.
The sun and moon watch while I weave your name;
The sun and moon hear while I count your name.
These are the wages I get by day and night
To deposit in the lotus bank of my heart.
I weave your name on the loom of my mind

To clean and soften ten thousand threads
And to comb the twists and knots of my thoughts.
No more shall I weave a garment of pain.
For you have come to me, drawn by my weaving,
Ceaselessly weaving your name on the loom of my mind.
(Weaving your Name by Kabir from *God Makes the Rivers to Flow: Sacred Literature of the World* Selected by Eknath Easwaran, founder of the Blue Mountain Center of Meditation, copyright 1991, 2008; reprinted by permission of Nilgiri Press, P. O. Box 256, Tomales, CA 94971, www.bmcm.org)

Breath control and breath focus lead us ever inward towards refining our spiritual being by combing out the knots of karma and resistance until every thread is 'singing' to higher and higher states of being. Much like a finely tuned musical instrument, we learn to express our inner soul song in harmony with all that is. We become mindful that we are a spiritual being having a human existence. This earth-bound form is not us. It is merely a vehicle and habitation. Identifying with this form as if it were you, is to limit your spirit to inhabiting a heavy cage. The assigned role of this body-vehicle is to allow us to express our spirituality through all the challenges of a human experience. Remembering to breathe consciously softens the mind-bonds to the physical body and reminds us that spirit is who we are. Breathing consciously draws our attention and indicates when we are expressing through irritation and not gentleness.

In the Sermon on the Mount, Jesus Christ proclaimed to the multitudes:

Blessed are the pure in heart for they shall see God.
(Matthew 5:8)

Let us remember that ever-increasing gentleness comes from purifying the heart, one breath at a time.

In this chapter, we will be learning to refine the breath to express gentleness through conscious attention and fineness of focus.

Right from the start in developing breath focus, we are faced with the arising of our own irritations. Know that these irritations are not you. If it is not deep peace and love that you find arising, know that this is just old karma and a false identity of self. Learn to retain your focus only on the purifying breath, gently scouring away the grime of the karma. One gentle breath at a time.

Hold onto the concept of anything that is not your bliss-filled God-self as ego-stuff: interwoven fibres of beliefs; locked in emotionally charged events and karma. Fibres, much like tangled threads in a sewing basket, link you to all the souls which you wronged, or believed you wronged. Fibres also tie you to the wheel of karma to release and forgive both yourself and other souls. Through karmic fibres, lifetime after lifetime, you are bound to relive the same situations and trials until one person 'wakes up' and realises that he or she can change this repeating pattern. This is always achieved by being gentle and loving: by forgiving wrongs. A hundred years from now, the history that you have lived through, will be just that: history. A narrative in the drama of life. This time round you may have played the role of a king. Another time you may have been a servant. You may be playing the role of husband, wife, sister, mother, father, brother, friend, business associate, grandparent. Realise that the role that you have chosen to play is perfect for what you came to learn. And ultimately, it is within us to wake up from earthly reality and to realise that you are none of these roles. It is merely the narrative that you find yourself playing in the most spiritually conscious way that you can. It is *how* you play your role without being too identified with it that matters. How do you express and embody God-qualities in all that you think, say and do? And are you developing, out with identification with earthly roles, your primary relationship beyond time and space, which is with God?

We learn to release identification with role in the earth drama by focusing on breathing. Become conscious that through breath, you can clean and soften the knots of threads of attachment, one conscious breath at a time.

Viloma Pranayama (Cutting the Inhale)

In cutting the inhale through *viloma pranayama* (see chapter16) we have the opportunity to explore the spaces between breaths. In the pauses, we become more attuned to our inner soul Self, sitting behind the breath. The breath is the bridge between the physical and the spiritual realms of awareness. By consciously bringing attention to the breath, we can glimpse a more and more finely attuned way, another more gentle state of being beyond earthly consciousness.

Conscious breathing is the gateway to God-consciousness, one conscious breath at a time. Viewed like this, it becomes obvious that we could start to tune into the breath anywhere and at anytime: on the bus, walking the dog, cleaning the toilet, brushing your teeth, etc. Rein in the thought processes and tune into the breath, wherever you happen to be. Can you follow the breath for one breath? One full inhale and exhale? Exhaling right to the last puff of air in the lungs? Each consciously breathed breath is one tiny step towards clearing old karma.

Take the attention to the breath. Observe the softness and evenness of the breath.

Extend the exhale, retaining soft, even focus right to the last puff of the exhale. Repeat for a few breaths.

Imagine stroking down a silk ribbon of Gentleness on the exhale. Have attention on even rhythm. Start to visualise stroking the ribbon of Gentleness with the start of the exhale and end the exhale beyond the threads of the ribbon. Repeat for a few breaths.

Create pauses in the inhale by 'cutting the breath' i.e. breathe in, pause, breathe in, pause, breathe in, pause. Hold attention on amplifying the quality of gentleness on each pause. Exhale, visualise smoothing the ribbon of Gentleness to the last thread. Repeat for several breaths.

Allow finer and finer expression of Gentleness with each breath.

Meditation on Gentleness

Connect with the golden heart of the Earth by linking roots down from the four petals of the base chakra (*muladhara*). Concentrate on letting roots be equally balanced left and right, front and back: letting down from all four petals of the base chakra.

Tune into the frequency of motherly gentleness of the Earth as she only seeks to nurture us, no matter how humankind might ravage the surface, she knows that this is all in Divine Order and accepts all unconditionally.

Golden light flows up our hollow spinal tube from the Earth star to connect with the centre of the head. Pure white light flows down from above the crown, linking us to a higher state of being.

Take your awareness to the belly, which softly expands on the inhale and relaxes on the exhale. Imagine that the sea within the belly has become calm. Visualise that deep beneath the surface there is an Ocean of Stillness. Feel into that deep stillness. Let that stillness become so intense that you encompass the whole ocean.

Visualise a still white flame. Imagine that it is continuously burning with a still intensity in the Cathedral of the Heart. In this vaulted, elevated space, your heart flame burns brightly, unsullied by time or place. Meditate on the still, white flame within.

Imagine reverently approaching the altar. Lay as an offering your earthly perception of the quality of gentleness and all that gentleness means to you. Recall a time when you were gentle with a child or animal. Lay that feeling-ness or memory on the altar.

Receive in its stead, the heavenly quality of Gentleness as the heavens open to fill you with Divine blessing. Heavenly Gentleness is the highest expression of love.

All sense of the cathedral and of earthly form falls away.

Experience being spirit: pure bliss and formlessness.

Float in nothingness as pure spirit.

See your earthly form as if from afar, as nothing more than your earthly vehicle.

Realise that physical death is simply releasing the physical body to live as pure spirit.

Release fear of bodily death and all limitation as an offering into the River of Life. Let that burden slip gently from your willing hands to be swept away in the current.

Allow your spirit to flow freely with the current of life.

Experience gentleness in the water, gentleness in its current and gentleness in your soul.

Know that all is well. All is in tune with Divine order.

Visualise pouring your soul into the spiritual body, then the mental body, the emotional body, the astral body and the etheric body. Resume the physical form with a new sense of peace.

Affirmation

I am pure spirit. I express gentleness of the Divine Mother as I work.

Chapter 19

Modesty (*hrir*)

The language of battle is often found in the scriptures, for it conveys the strenuous, long, drawn-out campaign we must wage to free ourselves from the tyranny of the ego, the cause of all our suffering and sorrow.
(From *The End of Sorrow: The Bhagavad Gita for Daily Living* by Eknath Easwaran, by kind permission of Nilgris Press)

Modesty is the quiet voice of shame or humility which lets us know when we have over-stepped the spiritual mark and carries with it the willingness to rectify mistakes. The voice of our conscience can be drowned out by the harsh clamour of brashness for attention, ego-indulgence and spiritual pride in ego's achievements. Know that a spiritual warrior is not boastful or brazen in showing off levels of attainment in spiritual prowess.

In the quiet stillness of spirit much soul magnetism is built, like a mansion around us, but harsh language or thoughts erode or shatter peace so that the spiritual aspirant must start building from scratch. At some time, we will learn that quiet magnetism is to be contained to help us remain in communion with God. Like a hole in a sack of corn, soul magnetism can trickle away slowly with restless thoughts or suddenly if we indulge in idle gossip or let anger rule over control. You will know what I'm talking about: feeling lighter than air after sitting quietly in deep meditation, you come down to gross physical existence with a bang if you let past-remarkableness have free rein. A guarded tongue allows us to taste the gravity or weight of our words before these are uttered. Not only are idle words harmful to others, these are etched in our own soul until we can learn to forgive ourselves and to guard words and thoughts.

Modesty is not just in word but in deed. I would like to tell you a story.

Once there was a very fast flowing river that rushed headlong over the rocks. It knew no fear as it powered and thundered through canyons and tumbled over all obstacles in its path. But one day the rains upstream did not come and the power of the river dwindled to a trickle. 'Why am I so weak?' asked the river. 'What am I without my force?'

And the heavens answered: 'It is we who give you your power for we hold the power of the rain.' And the river was finally humbled. It felt the cycle of the flow much more acutely in the softness of the trickle as it smoothed its way between the boulders of the drying river bed.

The moral of this story is: don't be in a rush to find the next entertainment, the next relationship or desire-driven goal, expending all your energies on the next and the next. Instead find solace in the steadiness of stable roots within the earth. The rush disguises the warring factions underneath the surface veneer of ego. In humility, we can finally expose the seeds that need uprooting so that the river can flow once more.

Furthermore, in the depth of meditation, cosmic knowledge is revealed to the sincere spiritual seeker. Each kernel of truth which is gifted to the soul has been sincerely won through spiritual perseverance, courage and faith. Is this kernel of truth to then be given away lightly to those who are not spiritual seekers or whom your conscience will let you know, are not genuine in asking? This would just lay us open to unnecessary ridicule. Would Jesus have told his truths to all and sundry? In fact Jesus, in His wisdom, knew that not everyone was ready to hear the whole truth or there were those who would persecute Him and His disciples for it. The parables were the vehicle of telling pretty moral tales for the masses with layers upon layers of meaning for those who had the ears to hear the wisdom.

The yogi of perfected wisdom should not bewilder the minds of men who have imperfect understanding. Deluded by the attributes of Nature, the ignorant must cling to the activities engendered by those gunas.
(Bhagavad Gita 3:29)

The secret is not to reveal to anyone the insights and truths which you experience. These are a private matter between you and God. If you hold these in the silence, the depth of wisdom contained therein will be revealed further. Do not be in a hurry to 'show off' each learning to even your closest friends until you have actualised that knowledge within: until it becomes soul knowledge. That takes time in the quiet. A master or guru might share his actualised knowledge but you can be assured that he has spent intense periods of silence until he IS the knowledge. If you have perception of the knowledge (what is known), knowing and the knower (you) as separate, then you have not yet attained soul mastery. The person who has attained self-realisation knows that he is not this body, and honour, dishonour or anything pertaining to this body is useless. To get in touch with your true self, you have to let go of the ego, which will present itself in increasingly subtle forms as you let go of one veil of unreality after another. The yogi must be diligent in extracting ego attachment as the motive behind each thought or deed.

Neither should we quietly bask in pride of soul knowledge. For in reality we have nothing. Everything is a gift from the divine: this body is not ours, the mind is not ours, indeed all knowledge is not ours either. We own nothing. So keep your wisdom hidden, until your quiet voice of conscience tells you that the person is ready to hear.

Neither should we be brazen in behaviour. Whose attention is it we seek in immodest behaviour and why? Ask yourself: will that serve me spiritually? If you catch yourself wondering if others approve, you'll know what I mean. We have all come a long way from seeking reward and feedback from the souls in our earthly drama. The spiritual warrior knows that none of these people can give him the peace and bliss which compare to living in God-consciousness. However, you may still have threads of attachment to looking for reaction (positive or negative) from others. Modesty is the quiet middle-path between extremes of behaviour which guides us to withdraw attachments into ever quieter and more sincere connection with God who is the sole agent of all actions, who is the source of all knowledge and soul reward of ever-new bliss.

In this chapter, we will be letting go of small threads of ego's expectation that others will respond in a certain way and from attention-seeking behaviour. We will learn how to listen in the quiet to the small voice of humility as the voice of your conscience, letting you know when you have committed even the smallest wrong. The spiritual path is like a knife edge: ever increasingly fine choices between spiritually right or wrong thought, word or action. Were it not for the quiet voice of shame or humility, we would be as blind-folded on the knife edge path. Indeed if we ever find ourselves blind to the path, we can have faith in the quiet guidance of conscience as our unerring guide.

Prayer

Oh Lord, guide me. I am not this body. I am not this mind. I am not drama of this incarnation. I am not the astral body. Reveal to me through the quiet voice of conscience who Thou art.

Circular Breathing into the Heart

Sit with the body comfortable and back erect.

Breathe into the heart.

Feel the softness of the breath either side of the heart.

Inhale, pause, soft exhale and pause before breathing in again.

Establish an equal ratio breath around the heart: Breathe in for a count of 4, hold for 4, breathe out for 4 and pause for 4.

Allow there to be a smooth transition between the four phases of the breath.

Focus on the breath being so smooth that there are no corners between each phase.

Merely a soft pause in the breath and then let the breath shift again. Just like tapping the brake pedal then softly release it again with the barest of pauses.

That is to say that the pauses are still the same length, but the quality of repress and release of the breath is increasingly subtle.

Note areas where the breath is smooth.

Note where your smooth focus is comprised of restlessness within. Seek to bring smoothness to the whole breath.

Have the breath so smooth that you breathe in a circle around the heart.

Let there be no perceptible end to the inhale or exhale and the start of each pause.

Hand over to God any raggedness of the breath.

Continue to focus on smoothly breathing in a circle.

Meditation on Letting Go of Attachment

Become still and quiet within.

Let go of behaviours that no longer serve you spiritually downwards into the bright light of a holy place in the earth.

Let your roots flow down also and bathe in the bright spiritual light of the earth. Be grateful for all the many ways that the earth nurtures and supports your physical form so that you may walk this earthly lesson.

Rest in the Earth's loving presence until you feel an answering warmth flowing upwards through the spine. Pure light ignites and clears each chakra in turn, filling the spiritual spine with light and colour and sound.

Gaze softly towards the spiritual eye in the inside of the brow.

Gaze softly upwards to the radiance of the many white petals of the crown chakra. Bathe in its spiritual light.

Be aware of being with God. Bask in His love.

Hand over any behaviours that bring you shame at the feet of God.

Allow the grace of God to wipe clean the slate of wrongs, absolving you of all ills.

Let your love and gratitude for God shine all the greater.

Be aware of being a sphere of white light. Nothing else exists but you and God.

When you are ready to return, map your awareness out into physical limbs and head once more. Slowly take up the physical senses once more.

Step by step, one quality at a time, we are learning to walk the inroad to a deeper, more fulfilling relationship with God. It may be helpful to record your awakening consciousness in a journal as a marker to recall those precious moments of divine connection to be re-read on those times when divine connection is harder to attain. There will be times when we will be required to put in greater effort as the path becomes ever narrower, so that we demonstrate our sincerity to God but also so that we can build the capacity to withstand the greater and greater magnitude of light as we continue on the spiritual path. It can be helpful to tap into that earlier moment to sustain us through the times when we meditate through faith alone.

Mantra

I am the way, the truth and the life.

Chapter 20

Lack of Restlessness (*achapalam*)

I know the path is strait and narrow.
It is like the edge of a sword.
I rejoice to walk on it. I weep when I slip.
God's word is: 'He who strives never perishes.'
I have implicit faith in that promise.
Though from my weakness I fail a thousand times,
I shall not lose faith.

(Mahatma Gandhi from *God Makes the Rivers to Flow: Sacred Literature of the World* Selected by Eknath Easwaran, founder of the Blue Mountain Center of Meditation, copyright 1991, 2008; reprinted by permission of Nilgiri Press, P. O. Box 256, Tomales, CA 94971, www.bmcm.org)

The path of enlightenment is fraught with many trials in the form of restlessness. Constancy is the hallmark of a spiritually strong yogi, neither swept by strong highs or lows but charting the quiet middle course, like a flat line on an ECG. We cannot be too harsh with ourselves when we fail from this ideal: simply dust ourselves off and endeavour to try again. For many attempts are needed to iron out even subtle inner restlessness.

Restlessness comes from three sources: emotional, mental and physical.

Emotional restlessness consumes us with amplified passions or desires. Perhaps there is a haunting undercurrent of grief for all things past. When you catch yourself lamenting small trinkets, remember that you have been promised the greatest of treasures. Do not be deceived by shiny baubles and homely comforts and led astray from the path towards enlightenment. Transient treasures are an earthly lure which have no appeal once one has tasted the ever-new, ever-lasting bliss of God-realisation. So, hold yourself quietly and with calm grace to the long run. But hear me when I say, do not grieve for any man, woman, position or material thing for has God not promised that you will receive greater in heaven? For is it not written:

> But seek ye first the kingdom of God, and his righteousness; and all these things shall be added unto you.
> (Matthew 6:33)

Mental restlessness is to be continually distracted by errant thoughts. Make up your mind to no longer pay attention to the next train of thought. In the station of Rest, simply do not let the Thought Train arrive in your quiet station. Settle down the mind state into peace and calm. Let no thoughts of unrest ruffle the waters of your mind. Take this, as in all things, as a test of your resolve. How much are you prepared to resist the process of enlightenment by warring within yourself? Is there a quiet to be found within acceptance? Perhaps you will find that the fight is within and not without.

Physical restlessness drives us to move the physical body and resists sitting immobile while in meditation. Choose to eliminate responding to the urge to scratch, twitch or move the eyes behind the lids. A short period of physical yoga prior to sitting for meditation is very beneficial in training the body-mind to sit still. Another method is to tense and relax each muscle group of the body, starting with the feet and legs and ending with screwing up the face, eyes tight shut, and relaxing into the scalp. Even if your limbs 'go to sleep' let them. Note any ego mental reactions to the reduced feedback from the physical body and seek to eliminate those reactions. Even the slightest twitch of a finger sets up a sound vibration in the aura which distracts us from the goal of transcendence of the human body-cage.

Eventually, as each physical sensation lulls into nonawareness, only the breath is left moving in the body. This is why the breath is the snare tethering us to *maya* (illusion) but if you persevere, eventually the breath will also become still. A Breathless State naturally arises when you have succeeded in stilling all three forms of restlessness which may last several minutes. Do not be alarmed (as this is a form of restlessness) for the body has no need to breathe at that moment and will naturally start to breathe again normally when it needs. This is not to be confused with 'holding one's breath', which is a conscious effort. The arrival of the breathless state is an indication that you are moving into a deeper state of spiritual consciousness. At this time, we find that we are being supported by something other than the breath. In the absence of physical breathing, we find a lightness within that is the rising of prana within the physical and astral bodies into pure consciousness within. Advanced yogis can cease the breath and the heartbeat at will when they have mastered sustaining the physical body on subtle *prana* (life force), drawn in through the medulla oblongata (the mouth of God).

Any of these can be experienced by the serious meditator, and we can feel besieged, to varying degrees of restlessness, at anytime except the final stage of full realisation, *Samadhi*, as mentioned by Patanjali (p. 7). As one releases veil after veil of what one is not, to reveal successively subtle attachments to family members, outer and inner faculties, it is common to feel apprehension about the new ecstatic states of contact with God which one is moving toward.

> *It is ridiculous for a person to fear that his various powers will be annihilated by entering the superior ecstatic state of God-union, as it would be to fear the extinction of any of his powers by their nightly state of suspended animation in sleep.*
> (Parmahansa Yogananda, *God Talks with Arjuna: The Bhagavad Gita* p. 159)

He is not born nor does He ever die; after having been, He again ceases not to be. Unborn, eternal, changeless and ancient, He is not killed when the body is killed.
(Bhagavad Gita 2:20)

One learns to treat this existential fear also as a form of restlessness. The path to reveal the Self becomes ever narrower between what is right (for you at that stage) and wrong. Any subtle restlessness must be traced back to its thread of physical or emotional attachment and let go. The importance of choosing wisely increases moment to moment. But be assured that you are progressing in just the right way for you at this time: slowly, steadily, keeping on with your meditation practice.

But don't confuse lack of action as lack of restlessness. A state of inaction can be inertia and sluggishness (*tamas*) unless you are consciously engaged in outward spiritual acts or inward god-focused meditation. The Gita advises us on taking a path of spiritual action.

Perform action, being steadfast in Yoga abandoning attachment and balanced in success and failure. Evenness of mind is Yoga.
(Bhagavad Gita 2:48)

We cannot simply refrain from action and lapse into the blissful actionless state. We have incarnated in this world and must act. Even breathing is an action. Through conscious actions, we remember to be in the world but not of the world. The state of inaction is only achieved after much sincere effort, commitment and whole-heartedly loving God so much that you have let go of your little ego-self. Your earthly responsibilities are, instead, your starting point for changing how you act and interact in this world. Remember that nothing is chance. Whatever you find yourself facing in the earth-drama is where you start. Continue even more fervently with your meditation practice until it takes you into the deeper awareness, where you will have a growing distance from identification with your particular role in the earth drama for this incarnation and an ever-deepening, finely tuned awareness of the love-bliss state of God consciousness.

So, we learn that sometimes it is not what we do, but the spirit from which we approach each action. Once, when I was ten years old, I visited Sami Ling Buddhist monastery at Eskdalemuir in the Scottish Borders. I was struck by the simplicity of monastic living and the beauty of Divine-absorption and worship within each simple daily task. I had a long conversation with one of the saffron-robed monks about how every moment is potentially charged with God-consciousness: we merely need to be present and to show up. What he imparted to me, and even the vibration of his words, electrically charged me so that decades later, that one moment is indelibly etched in the ethers. And so now I invite you to 'show up' in the present moment. To be awake. Let's look at a small mundane task: can you be 100 per cent present in simple tasks such as washing one dish, recycling waste or feeding a pet? Deliberately choose tasks of short duration, of a minute. Your aim is to be present in cleaning the dish for God, responsibly blessing the waste or loving your pet, without letting any other deviation of thought or emotion intrude. You might make a list of tasks and record how successful you were in being lovingly conscious of acting for God. You might use affirmation to aid the focus:

God, I wash this cup in order that you may bless my action and fill me with your wisdom.
Divine Father, I am grateful for your bounties and I recycle these materials with gratitude for their use.
Divine Mother, as you bless all souls with Motherly love so do I love and care for my pet.

An affirmation acknowledging the divine aid which is available at all times helps to place us in the flow of that love and wisdom. As in all tools, they are an aid on the spiritual path until such times as, in single-pointed God-focus, all need of affirmation to focus the mind-emotion will simply fall away in unwavering absorption in God. Until such times, use the breath focus and mental affirmation to help 'hold' the mind with the intention of pleasing God with the simple task at hand.

Therefore we learn to discriminate God-conscious acts with those where our mind ran away with itself on another track entirely. In those moments we are not present. At the end of each day, reflect on the moments that were focused on being truly conscious of acting for God and as God in this world. (Do not focus on the moments where the day ran away with itself and where you 'fell asleep' within your incarnational role. In those moments you forgot that you're playing a role in the soap opera of earthly life and not to take it too seriously. And certainly don't beat yourself up for going off piste, for that only makes a restless mind and raging emotions even more entrenched.) It is in the small moments of the day that you can establish your private adoration of God, expressed through the most mundane of tasks. Could you even relish the tasks which you avoid and choose instead to target those as an offering to God? Using a repeated mantra will detach you from negative emotional attachment to the task: *'Lord, with this act, I glorify you.'*

Ultimately, as we relinquish the false belief that it is we who act, we realise that God is the sole doer of any action. It is the Creator who in the ever-expanding act of creation is the divine actor, the act and the creation. God is continually holding our created soul in the vast tapestry of all that is. Through *Aum*, the sound of creation, He is continually 'singing' the life force which sustains you and your physical body within creation through the medulla oblongata at the back of the head. Once you perceive that cosmic vibration as a rushing or roaring sound at the back of the head, you have a conscious realisation that you are not the agent in this body. It is God who sustains both this physical vehicle and our soul with life force (*prana*), both directly through cosmic sound and indirectly through sunlight, food, water and fresh air.

Progressing deeper and deeper in meditation, we loosen the ties of belief that it is we who act at all. When we think that it is we who do any action, we have become blindfolded by the illusion of God's mystical creation which is there to help us go within, to find the golden thread or the trail of cosmic breadcrumbs to find our way out of the forest of *maya*. That's why it is so important to use a period of daily discernment to attune within to a higher vibration state when we remember to consciously act during those small mundane daily tasks. Step by step, we attune to the cosmic reality. Perhaps you will have sudden flashes of intuition when you see a glimpse of God's grand cosmic plan. Or perhaps you don't. Dear hearts, it doesn't matter whether you receive signals that you are in the right direction or not, just keep on, keeping on: steadily and surely, handing over action after action to God as recognition and gratitude that we are agents for the divine. Then we turn inwards towards knowing God as firsthand, ever-new bliss in our hearts.

Spiritual action is to live the dual experience of being in the world but not of the world. Realise that you are God, not the action, nor the body which acts. Since all creative life force comes from God, it is foolish to believe that it is we who act at all. When we consciously become as the Father in the vibration-less void beyond and behind creation while still in the physical body, we detach from attachment to sense desires and bodily senses, realising that all other is 'that which is not I'. Pray continually for the Father to reveal his/herself behind the illusion of creation: 'Father, reveal thyself!'

Nadi Shodhanam Pranayama (Alternate nostril breath)

Stage three: Tuck in the fingers (as on p. 50), starting with the left nostril (spiritual side of the body). Perform 16 rounds with the intent to increase the length of the breath retentions after the exhale and then the inhale. The ratio below can be extended by keeping the same ratio to 12:12:12:12, 20:20:20:20 for instance.

Inhale	Hold	Exhale	Hold
4	4	8	4 for 4 rounds
4	4	8	8 for 4 rounds
4	8	8	8 for 4 rounds
8	8	8	8 for 4 rounds

Then let the breath return to its natural cycle. Notice the smooth quality of the breath and how much restlessness has fallen away after the discipline of the natural breath in the practice above.

Meditation: Sitting within the Square

Imagine sitting immobile within a square doorway, perfectly balanced between left and right, neither allowing thoughts to pull us backward into the past, or forward into the future. Having a mental thought frame can help us as a stage in the process of allowing the body to be still, for as it settles into immobility, we find that only the breath moves the body. The breath relaxes into a softness which can barely be felt or heard. At some point, a restless urge to move the body will become apparent or even overwhelming. If we do not move the body, the ego-mind loses sense of a map within space. The mental construct of the doorway is an aid to being mentally and emotionally comfortable with the ego compliant within your inner journey to calmness.

Ground your roots into the earth, letting go of inner resistance to spiritual progress.

Attune to the highest, brightest star above your head, to a higher frequency entrainment.

Observe the breath, following the journey of the inhale and the soft, long exhale.

As awareness of the physical body recedes, allow the imaginary boundary of the mental square to serve you as a framework of delineation of self.

Withdraw consciousness to the centre of the square. Sit motionless, except for the softest of breaths within the centre. Focus intent, thought and will and practise being actively calm.

Imagine sitting within the square doorway, with the uprights either side of the body and the lintel above your head. Fine tune and control the mind to stay within the narrow confines of the centre of the square. Withdraw into the very centre.

If the mind deviates, re-route the Thought Train by affirming: 'this train does not stop here. I am sitting still. I am meditating.' Use the soft breath to breathe away any restlessness that arises.

Prayer

Divine Father, I lay all restlessness at Your feet. Fill me with deep rest and stillness so that I may perceive Your true glory.

Chapter 21

Vigour (*tejas*)

Just as the single sun illuminates the whole world, the sole Knower of the field lights up the entire field. All beings, great and small, saint and sinner, high and low, get their light – their consciousness – from this one source.
(Jack Hawley, *The Bhagavad Gita: A Walkthrough for Westerners*, 13:33)

We are each created with our unique soul light merged in divine harmony and Oneness with the whole of creation. In bliss, we only knew bliss. How could we truly know bliss unless we had known (seemingly) other than bliss? And so we chose to incarnate in illusory causal, astral and physical bodies, as successively dense veils covering the light within that we might truly realise ourselves as God. The journey of enlightenment is to awaken to the reality of highest expression of our divine inner radiance, a spiritual light.

Spiritual radiance or vigour is revealed by persistent stripping away of what we are not, layer by limiting layer, to realise the great 'I am' light within.

First, we must transcend the physical body by releasing all erroneous attachments and beliefs that we are the visible body, any of the character traits, or roles. For we are none of these. Feedback from the five senses, if perceived as real, keeps us tied into the limiting experience as a human vehicle lifetime after lifetime. As yogis, we learn to withdraw attachment to anything in the illusory physical world and from attachment to the illusory physical vessel. Without the five senses there is no feedback to the ego of physical extremities. We can learn to pull back awareness from each sense, through control of the breath and focus on the spiritual eye or brow (*ajna*) chakra, which is also called the centre of Christ Consciousness.

If therefore thine eye be single, thy whole body shall be full of light.
(Matthew 6:22)

We can 'see' with inner astral sight, when we withdraw 'seeingness' from the two physical eyes along the optic nerves. Let the level of your gaze be from the level of the brow (spiritual eye) inside of the head, gazing intensely with unwavering focus.

The process of vanquishing the mind and senses consists of shutting out the external world, focussing one's gaze on the centre of spiritual consciousness between the eyebrows, and gradually equalising the in-going and out-going breath. Then, when the body, mind, senses and intellect are under control (without desire, fear and anger), realisation of the constant freedom and bliss within the Godhead comes.
(Jack Hawley, *The Bhagavad Gita: A Walkthrough for Westerners*, 5:27-28)

Through intensity of focus, the spiritual eye reveals that the body is formed of light. The flesh is a patterning of light currents and an even more subtle astral body is visible as even finer currents of *prana.* Beyond the astral body and its fine nerves (nadis), an advanced yogi can see the even finer causal body. Handing over every attachment to the physical can be extremely challenging: that's when the ego throws up all manner of distractions and fears. Remember the ego isn't real: it's the illusory self. Learn instead to tune into the God within and love Him with all your heart and soul. Love is the language of God. The more intensely devotional you are, offering all that you are, including the in-breath and the out-breath, by Divine Grace, the ego-limitation is dissolved. Through selflessness and Divine Love you learn to trust placing all your eggs in God's basket: the physical, the astral and the causal.

The process of Self Realisation is to reveal our True Nature as Light. When we have perfected meditation, simply letting go of all seeming separateness, our consciousness merges with the Creator. Dissolving the physical body illusion into the astral body illusion, the astral body into the causal body illusion and transcending all three planes of existence, one becomes as a radiant golden fire. *Tejas* is a shining radiance and fire that comes from within, cultivated through sincere spiritual practice, until our aura is burning like a 200-watt bulb.

In *Samadhi*, we can perceive the same Light essence within all things as vibrating pure life energy.

It is the Spirit of God that actively sustains every form and force in the universe; yet He is transcendental and aloof in the blissful uncreated void beyond the worlds of vibratory phenomena.
(Sri Yukteswar cited in Paramahansa Yogananda, *Autobiography of a Yogi*)

Everywhere we look in the natural world, there is beauty and radiance to be found in the most ordinary of situations: from a tenacious dandelion breaking through concrete to a shaft of sunlight through trees. Sometimes you might find yourself struck dumb with awe and wonder at the beauty all around. In those extraordinary, everyday occurrences, we are continually reminded that our soul journey is to shine brightly. When we learn to radiate light in meditation, to the exclusion of everything else, we will have learned to vibrate and amplify our unique soul vibration for the pure joy of being awake and aware in God's infinite ocean of peace.

Our soul essence is our centre-most nature, untouched by time or circumstance. It is the God-spark within our hearts. By long, intense periods of meditation on God, we develop our soul magnetism as an aura of goodness and a quiet outer expression of deep inner joy. When all that is not your essence is peeled away, it is that radiance of character which remains. St Paul expressed it as:

> *For now we see through a glass, darkly; but then face to face: now I know in part; but then shall I know even as also I am known.*
> (1 Corinthians 13:12)

That inner radiance cannot be seen clearly or realised until the grim and dusty karma of many lifetimes is cleared by sincere spiritual practice and breath control.

Pranayama: Learning to breathe *prana*

Allow the breath to be feather light. Watch the passage of breath as it travels on the inhale through the nose and throat and into the lungs and the feather light passage of the out-breath. Stay with the breath, becoming hyper aware of subtle fluctuations in the mind-quality with which we approach the breath.

Move behind the physical breath. Bring a devotional quality to the breath.

Offer up the inhale into the exhale.

Offer the exhale into the inhale.

Become conscious of breathing something more subtle than air, that the breath is sustaining you beyond the need for oxygen. You are held and sustained by greater than the breath. Keep offering ownership of the breath until you are breathing *prana*.

A natural breathless state may arrive. Pauses between breathing may come and go.

Offer the inhale into the exhale as the highest of offerings. Pour the exhale into the inhale. Release any hold on 'grasping' the inhale or exhale.

Allow the breath to be an offering unto itself. Your breath is the closest that you have to your spiritual consciousness, so offer that breath as a blessing on your spiritual unfolding: offer the inhale into the exhale and the exhale into the inhale.

Release owning the breath. In reality, even the air is a gift from God. Offer it back unto God as the highest blessing that you can bestow.

Meditation: Moving beyond Physical Identity

Bring your gaze to the inside of the spiritual eye.

Perceive that just in front of you, through the spiritual eye, is the patterned curtain of existence, the cosmic illusion or *maya*. On this side of the curtain, you perceive this temporal world as reality; when in reality, experiencing Oneness of being is just beyond that curtain.

Ask yourself: what keeps you bound here?

Through the breath offer up all resistance or reactions to this practice to God.

With infinite patience stay with the breath as the start of the bridge to truly knowing God.

You may be able to perceive a rise in the *prana* in the astral spine on the inhale and a descent on the exhale.

Continue to offer the breath: offering inhale into the exhale; exhale into the inhale.

Prayer

'Divine Father, awaken Thy wisdom within me that I may realise Thy Cosmic Light within all of creation.'

Chapter 22

Forgiveness (*kshama*)

Father, forgive them for they know not what they do.
(Luke 23:34)

Jesus' perfect mission on Earth was to teach us how to love, even those who seek to harm us. He demonstrated how to forgive and love even under perceived extreme physical suffering. Jesus' words were a prayer of forgiveness on the cross for those who cursed and put him to death. The deeper meaning of this plea was for all of humanity to wake up from the divine illusion: to realise the Divine Spirit within each other.

Forgiveness is the quality of the divine feminine which graciously allows others to be released from any ills that they may have done us and for us to graciously release ourselves from any ills which we have done to others. No matter how large, weighty and unforgiveable the issue may seem to be, seen from the perspective of the Divine Mother, everything is forgivable. The Divine Mother holds the greatest of loves and sees us all as errant children who, in the process of discerning right from wrong, will make some poor choices. Seen from a higher vibrational place, you can perhaps realise that while your choices were not always wise, learning to forgive yourself is the profoundly spiritual release.

When I was a child, I talked like a child, I thought like a child, I reasoned like a child. When I became a man, I set aside childish ways.
(1 Corinthians 13:11)

You were operating at the highest and best that you knew at that time. Hindsight is a great master, as it will offer better alternative pathways. However, at that time in your life path, you chose as wisely as you could. You need to extricate harsh judgement that others may have given you at the time, but the harshest judge of all will be yourself. How many times have you beaten yourself up for your actions? How many more self-beatings will be needed before you feel you have suffered enough? Will self-castigation assuage the guilt? Does it make you feel better? And most importantly, will it make you a better person in the eyes of God?

I suggest that the time for retribution of self is over. Well and truly over. Forgiveness and acceptance allows you to have respite from uselessly causing yourself endless pain through lifetime after lifetime.

God, through the OM vibration, is continuously guiding you home in bliss to everlasting Oneness in Spirit. All you need do is tune in and learn to deeply listen to that internal sound. I invite you to listen deeper than you have ever listened before. What if God were just about to reveal Himself to you in the next second? Then you may start to understand the level of expectancy, unwavering focus and intimacy that your listening will need to be.

Settle down the mind state into peace and calm.

Let no thoughts of unrest ruffle the waters of your mind.

Take whatever you are facing, as in all things, as a test of your resolve. How much are you prepared to resist the process of enlightenment by warring within yourself? Is there a quiet to be found in acceptance? Perhaps in your heart, you'll find that the fight is within and not without.

Can you lay down the gauntlet and forgive once and for all? Pray to God to fill you with forgiveness.

Know that in prayer, all of your questions have sailed within to the lips of God. God tastes your despair and pleasure, distrust or faithful prayer. Know that while these extremes still exist as a reality within you your little ego-identified character remains as a barrier to the glory that awaits you in Divine Oneness.

Be not afraid, for fear IS the barrier. Nothing exists with the outpouring of God's enduring love. Why, then, do you hesitate on the brink of conscious realisation when God has promised that it will be so? God has sent His heralds to guide you, in the form of Jesus Christ, Bhagavan Krishna, Mahavatar Babaji, Sai Baba, Paramahansa Yogananada and many other saints and masters, for their soul resonance is reverberating within this earthly realm. God so loves you that He has sent Divine dispensations now and always to welcome you back into the fold of His presence. Listen in your heart for it is yearning to be home.

As long as you believe yourself to be external to God's love, always looking in from the cold outside, that will be your continued experience. Why then, dear heart, do you persist in withholding yourself from Oneness?

Come, step away from your small ego-identified shell into God's Ocean of Bliss and taste the sweetness therein.

The Holy Spirit breathes and moves in you, continually beckoning you to this realisation. A surfeit of trust is the major barrier. Can you yet forgive? Lift the veil between these two states of being and see God in all appearance of duality: the persecutor and the persecuted; the good and the bad; the knowledgeable sage and the ignorant. No matter how deluded and far away from the truth we may seem, we are just a heart's beat from soul realisation, if we but knew it.

This is where fearlessness comes again to the fore. For the spiritual warrior is required to lose all that he or she identifies with as self, to let his or her true nature and soul radiance shine forth.

So, let your little cork of love float on God's Ocean of Calmness and find rest therein.

Rest from all clamouring and tussling of earthly life.

Become aware that every breath has a corresponding physical response in the body. You may be aware that the ribs rise and fall with the inhalation and exhalation. In this exercise, we will become attuned to the subtler responses both physically and energetically.

Breath Observation on the Body's Physical Responses

Take your awareness into the breath. Which has the most effort to the physical body – the inhalation or the exhalation? You will find that the inhalation requires a muscular action of the diaphragm to pull air into the lungs; the exhalation is only a reflex relaxation of the diaphragm returning to resting position.

Take your awareness now into the tail bone and pelvic floor. Breathe into the abdomen and tune into the answering response in this area of the physical body, and another response with the natural exhalation. Here we are not manipulating the breath, merely observing the natural changes occurring in the body with every breath. Breathe in, there is a slight increase in pressure in the coccyx – pelvic floor area. Breathe out and there's an answering response in the spinal fluid. The action of the breath is to cause a hydraulic pressure in the pelvic floor to shift it downwards as we breathe in and an upwards corresponding response in the spinal fluid on the exhale. Stay with this a few moments until your breath is consciously in tune with the pressure/release movements caused by simply breathing. Now, consciously energetically release with the exhale. Stay with this for a few breaths.

Lotus Meditation

Touch forefinger and thumb of each hand in the *jnnana* mudra.

Tune into the point of contact of skin on skin: left forefinger and thumb; right forefinger and thumb, as two bright lights.

Be aware of the brow as a third bright light, like three stars forming a triangle.

Sit with the perception of distinct bright lights until the rest of the physical body fades away.

Mentally perform *nadi shodhanam* (alternate nostril breath, see p. 43) but without moving the hands.

Keep awareness on the brow; breathe in a line of light from the right forefinger/thumb *mudra* (right hand immobile on the lap) to the brow. Retain the breath and focus on the brow. Breathe out a line of light from the brow to the left forefinger/thumb (left hand immobile on the lap).

Reverse the direction on the next inhale, from the left hand to the brow, sitting the focus of the pause in the breath on the brow, breathing out from the brow to the right forefinger/thumb.

Repeat for 12 rounds maintaining the focus of travelling from one star point to the next.

Continue for another 12 breaths by adding in a pause after each exhale, with the point of focus on the contact of skin on skin between each forefinger/thumb. Introduce an equal ratio 6:6:6:6.

Release the mental *nadi shodhanam* practice and take awareness to the two points of contact of the *mudras* in each hand, as a line of connection between two points of the triangle.

Notice what changes as you breathe in and as you breathe out. Imagine that there is a line between the two *mudra* stars that gets brighter as you breathe in and intensifies as you breathe out.

Breathe into the line of connection. Breathe out and release light into the hands.

Blessed are the merciful, for they shall receive mercy.
(Matthew 5:7)

Mercy is a stronger father's love to let you off the hook from continual eternal self-flagellations. Forgiveness is a mother's love and knows no bounds or judgements.

Imagine you are holding the qualities of Forgiveness in the

left hand and Mercy in the right.

Imagine your seated body was as a lotus: bulb and roots embedding in the deep dark silt, hidden from sunlight, in the nurturing nutrients and attached into the earth.

Stem growing upwards through the green dark waters into the sunlight of being.

Through forgiveness and mercy, let go at last.

And Shine.

Prayer

Divine Mother, fill me with Thy Divine radiance and goodness. Let me perceive thy radiance in all beings.

Chapter 23

Patience or Fortitude (*dhriti*)

To lose patience is to lose the battle.
(Gandhi)

Know that the breath is the bridge between the cosmic illusion (*maya*) which you can perceive through the senses playing out all around you and the true reality within. Staying with the breath with a calm, steady attention, we learn a deepening patience. The aim here is to notice any small irritations in the physical, mental or emotional states and simply wait until they pass. Think about the itch which suddenly develops on the cheek; if you let it have your attention it starts to scream at you to move and scratch it. But there is another way. Patience is calmly rerouting the attention to waiting. For the urge will pass. Intellectually, you know that there is nothing wrong, it's only an itch, right? Why then is the urge so all-pervasive and demanding that you move? The answer is that the ego seeks to urge us to move, for without feedback from bodily senses or emotional reaction, it ceases to exist. You are not this irritation. Neither are you the little ego-self.

Patience is the quality that allows us to *wait* out those 3 or 4 seconds, in quiet space outside irritation as part of the cosmic illusion, until it passes. Realise that in any moment you have a choice. Succumb to the illusion (take the blue pill) or choose to wake up (taking the red pill). In this chapter, we will be learning to exercise infinite patience. That is how we cross the bridge to the inner astral realm which is infinitely more vast, beautiful, enthralling and exists beyond time and space, which are only earthly constructs.

The good news is that we need only wait a few seconds until

each irritation goes. My legs used to 'shout' to me to move when I first started meditation. The ache of the legs going to sleep or the pins and needles sensation of the blood flowing back in was sheer agony. I applied intellectual knowledge to remind my ego-body that it wasn't being harmed. Learning to reroute attention somewhere else was the biggest lesson; thinking of touching the sea or a forest in my mind, for those seconds, until the urge to move passed helped.

Meditation is an army boot-camp for the spiritual seeker of God. Learning to bring the ego-soldier into line so that it responds without question and putting bodily discomforts to the side, is the training ground for acquiring infinite patience and stamina. If you let yourself be put off when the going gets tough, give yourself a good spiritual shake. Recall the spiritual masters and saints: none of them attained conscious self-realisation without intense periods of training in meditation. At the beginning, meditation quickly brings a sense of peace and opens up a world beyond the patterned curtain of earthly existence but deeper seated bodily and mental fluctuations will show up in time.

So merely pick yourself up and try, try, try again.

Pranayama Square Breath

Sama vritti (equal breath ratio) using a '*pranayama* square' focus. The *pranayama* square helps to maintain an equal breath ratio but can also help by giving an active mind something to focus on. The perfect geometry of the square brings a deep stability, a framework, whilst developing inner stability through Patience.

Imagine a square on your abdomen, starting at your left hip at the star.

Imagine through the breath, travelling in a star pinpoint of light, tracing a line from left hip to left lower rib.

Hold the breath as you imagine tracing a line from left rib to lower right rib.

Breathe out as you trace an imaginary line from right rib to

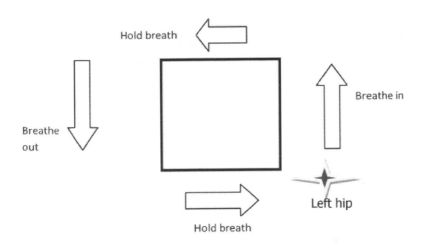

right hip.

Hold the breath as you trace line from right hip to left hip.

The focus is to stay with the journey of the star, travelling between the points of the square. Try not to allow your attention to jump to the next corner of the square but stay with the star, travelling at an even pace. At each corner, you may be aware of a solid 90^0 turn. Choreograph mentally travelling around the square, with the four parts of the breath: inhale, turn, pause, turn, exhale, turn, pause, turn and repeat.

Meditation

Sit still. Let a quietness rise from within.

Take awareness to the golden light at the centre of the Earth. Allow the golden light to flow upwards, filling the heart.

Take awareness to the pure, white star of the highest expression of your soul consciousness. Visualise pure, white light flowing in the vessel of the heart.

Allow the heart vessel to be filled to overflowing with the holy light of spirit.

Inhale steadily with focus on filling the heart with white light.

Hold the breath, intensifying the brightness of the white light (as long as the body naturally wants to, pause the breath).

Exhale so long and softly that there are no ripples within the white light contained in your heart vessel.

Stay with this breath for at least twelve breaths.

As the heart lightens, watch for any leaking of the Holy Light of Spirit as perforations in the heart vessel. Leakage is through attachment to anyone or anything (either holding onto pain or fear). Let go of any attachment. Instantly, the white light of spirit fills and heals all gaps.

In this divine blessing, be conscious that you have always been supported and guided and will always be so. Let go of any attachment to feeling unworthy.

Hand over unworthiness to God and replace with gratitude for all the unseen aid you have received.

Meditate on containing the Holy Light of Spirit in your heart vessel.

Touch the tongue to the soft palate or roof of the mouth.

Divine nectar (*amrita*) is continually flowing from the *bindi* point (crown of the hair) and dropping into the body. Catch these drips on your tongue as a vessel for *amrita*, before falling into the heart vessel.

Let the tongue rest. Take your awareness to the medulla oblongata (back of the head). Be aware of the flow of *prana* pouring in the back of the head as God is continually holding your body, mind and spirit in creation.

Allow the *prana* to flow in a channel of white light from the back of the head to the inside of the brow. Hold awareness for several breaths.

Be aware of *prana* reflecting back to the *bindi* point (at the crown of the hair). Hold awareness on the flow for several breaths.

From there, *prana* flows into the spine. The spine fills from the base chakra, filling each chakra in turn with light before spilling like a fountain of light into the one above until each chakra is brimming over with continually flowing light.

Be in the centre of the head, opening into a still space.
Let go of awareness of the edges of the skin.
There is only you and God.
Love God with all your soul.

Prayer

Father, reveal Thy mysteries to me.

Chapter 24

Cleanliness of Body and Purity of Mind and Heart (*shaucha*)

In this chapter, we will be exploring a physical and mental cleansing as a spiritual practice.

We can view the physical body as a God-given vessel where we can meet God within its hallowed walls. Daily washing of the body can be a holy ritual, as befitting a temple of God. Empty ritualistic cleansing as mere duty will not suffice: bathe consciously in the moment awareness of what you are doing and why you are doing it. Wash as an act of reverence and to please God. Each little action which is offered up to God, even the necessary ones of daily hygiene, where we are fully conscious and reverential, does not go unnoticed: they are marked in your auric field as motes of gold. Spiritualising small every day bodily ablutions, can make the mundane divine. Pretend, if needed, that God is witnessing your actions and *how you do them* from the inside, not as an external, judgemental paternal deity, but as your dearest, closest friend in your heart. Pretend that you are bathing God, not your body and you will come closer to the level of importance and magnificence that daily ablutions can be.

For cleansing the inside of the physical body, you may find, in certain seasons, a need for a cleaning fast or abstinence from certain foods. Some teachers suggest having a fast one day a week when we give the digestive process a rest. The breaking down of food to extract the *prana* and nutrients within it is a tiring process for the body. It also is a dampening, downwards pull away from the upward, lightening journey of *prana* through the spine. Taking a holiday from eating physical food allows one to dive deeply into meditation.

Cleansing of mind is most important: be vigilant for any errant thoughts and emotions which are harboured in the dark. Learn to bring the light into the dark recesses of the mind. Bring everything into the light for scrutiny and relinquishing. Leave no stone unturned in your quest to free the mind of all darkness and insecurities. Parmanahansa Yogananada's guru, Swami Sri Yukteswar, described the process of spiritual refinement from the state of *maya* (complete delusion) from 'the dark heart' to the propelled heart, to the steady heart, the devoted heart and finally, after diligent persistence and devotion, attaining the clean heart.

In the dark heart man misconceives: he thinks that this gross material portion of the creation is the only real substance in existence, and that there is nothing besides.
(Sri Yukteswar, *The Holy Science* 3:24)

The propelled heart motivates the seeker to wake up from the Cosmic Dream. Through immersion in the holy stream of light within, there arises a steady heart, abandoning the external world and becoming devoted to the internal one. In attaining the clean heart, ignorance is withdrawn and the heart becomes a clean slate devoid of all external ideas except the light of God as the real substance of creation.

Then man becomes able to comprehend the Spiritual Light, Brahma [spirit], the Real Substance in the universe.
(Sri Yukteswar, *The Holy Science*, 3:30)

Meditation on Clearing Insecurities

Visualise a pure white star above your head.

White light washes you clear of any belief in imperfection. See layers of gossamer shields in dull colours hiding your inner glory. White light strips away layer after layer of mis-held beliefs.

Feel pure white light filling the bones of the body: skull, chest, arms, hands. Spine, hips, legs and feet.

Visualise white light spiritualising the very bones of the body, charging them up until the bones dissolve into light.

Visualise running as a child in a heavenly garden full of birds of every hue from humming birds to birds of paradise. This garden is perfection. Here you meet all manner of elevated beings and angels.

You feel guided into a quiet nook in the garden where the Divine Mother is waiting for you. She lifts off layers of misconceptions and beliefs in imperfection, like lifting off clothing. Revealed is your shining light self in pure perfection.

The Divine Mother shows you a still pool of water, like a mirror, where you can see your soul perfection. She shows you your earthly body and the layers of insecurities which you armoured it with.

As you watch, she lifts layers of shielding from your earthly experience. It is like looking through a window onto your human life.

She lifts off all the weight and any identification with suffering from your earthly self, until your soul, in shining perfection, is revealed in shining perfection.

The mirror dissolves into light. You feel so light and weightless that you are able to run and jump without effort. Feeling as carefree as a child, you play in this heavenly garden. Experience a wellspring of joy bubbling over with joy of living.

Back in the physical, tune into the vibration of the white star above your head.

Raise your light body to sit within the star and bathe in white light.

Breathe in pure white light and exhale the being-ness of the heavenly garden. Experience it as a state of being, not a place.

Sit within white light.

Focus on gazing towards the brow, mentally chanting 'Om'.

Spiritualise the mind with pure white light, as a deep peace abides.

Mantra

I am that I am.

Prayer

Divine Mother, Cleanse my body and purify my mind as I offer Thee my devotion in the temple of my heart.

Chapter 25

Absence of Hate (*adroha*)

One believes he is the slayer, another believes he is the slain. Both
are ignorant: there is neither slayer nor slain. You were never born,
you will never die. You have never changed, you can never change.
Unborn, eternal, immutable, immemorial, you do not die when the
body dies. Realising that which is indestructible, eternal, unborn
and unchanging: how can you slay or cause another to slay?
(From *The Bhagavad Gita*, 2:19-21 translated by Eknath
Easwaran, founder of the Blue Mountain Center of Meditation,
copyright 1985, 2007; reprinted by permission of Nilgiri Press)

The boundary of skin is illusory. When we close our eyes and
remain completely still, the ego-identified boundary of the
physical body is no longer reality. In the absence of stimuli
from the nerves and physical senses, the ego becomes alarmed,
sending out random thoughts and urges to move. If you sit still
long enough the ego eventually gives up and becomes quiet, in
the same way that a dog which doesn't get attention will return
to its bed.

The path of Self-realisation is to slough off the illusion
of separateness and develop the power to see God in all. We
learn to see any heinous act as a result of a soul, in a belief of
separateness, experiencing suffering, unaware that at anytime
they are but a breath away from realising their true Reality in
Union with all that is. The soul is always perfect, although it
may be shrouded in many diaphanous veils of illusion.

As those on the spiritual path, we have a choice at any moment
to perpetuate the myth of separateness by speaking, thinking or
acting from hatred:

... nursing (her) wrath to keep it warm.
(Robert Burns, *Tam O'Shanter*)

Or we can make a concerted effort to rid ourselves of any harboured seeds of separateness and belief that physical skin is a boundary to consciousness. Trust that any perceived injustices that you may witness in the world operate exactly under God's karmic law, even if we do not at times understand.

It's coming yet for a' that,
That Man to Man, the world o'er,
Shall brothers be for a' that.
(Robert Burns, *A Man's a Man For A' That*)

Hate stems from belief that others have wronged you and an attachment to revenge, jealousy or malice. As those on the spiritual path, we have most likely been working on letting go of hate, knowing that it does no good. It is a buried cesspool of emotion which keeps us karmically bound to incarnation after incarnation, often, again to the same souls. And seeking intellectual answers or solutions is futile. In the end, the path comes to deep, quiet acceptance of all that is.

If you experience emotionally or physically suffering pain, your spiritual path is one of acceptance in partnership with detachment. An attachment to the pain you seem to be experiencing keeps it alive. That is to say, your consciousness is invested in living within the nub of pain, living it over and over in each new moment. Pain control comes from a mental and emotional release from attachment:

- To the pain itself as a reality here and now
- To the person or God whom you blame for it
- To the belief that you suffer: which is the 'you' that suffers? The immutable soul cannot be hurt

Deep-seated attachments are challenging to let go of, hence 'absence from hatred' is the penultimate of the twenty-six spiritual qualities. Pain can become a background. It's all a matter of choosing where you place your consciousness: in the pain or in with God. Experiencing extreme physical pain is a supreme test of your spiritual acumen and resolve.

Practise placing your awareness elsewhere so that you become mentally and spiritually strong, well versed in the technique when you are next anticipating pain. In the dentist's chair is a good example: you could place your awareness in the mouth, in the anticipation of pain or you could take your awareness beyond the physical into a meditative Oneness. Be in your inner moment not in anxious anticipation of pain. It is a matter of repeated practice until nothing ruffles your inner calm.

Perception of pain or illness is a choice. Place your awareness in meditation and let a belief in suffering and all its attachments to blame and hatred, simply fall away. A master, like Jesus, is able to detach from physical attachment, including what is commonly perceived as suffering.

The secret is in the attachment. What is at the end of the attached fibre of suffering?

In time, every thread and knot must be softened and released, even deeply held pernicious beliefs in being wronged. Let go of the kite-string. Realise that nothing can harm you; it is you who holds onto the harm. But that too is a choice. The soul cannot be hurt.

See God behind others' eyes. Ego challenges us with 'hate' in order to extract the fine subtle fibres of attachment to a belief in illusion of Duality (*maya*). The truth of Divine Union is the ultimate reality.

Love your enemies, bless them that curse you, do good to them that hate you, and pray for them which despitefully use you, and persecute you.
(Matthew 5:44)

Kappalabhati Pranayama

This *kriya* (cleansing) breath clears deep-seated *samskaras* (latent karmic tendencies). By pumping the pelvic floor and lower abdomen muscles with a sharp exhalation, *samskaras* stored within the lower three chakras are cleared. Hate is associated with the sacral chakra (*svadhistana*) and can be released by consciously operating from love within the heart (*anahata)* chakra whilst performing *kappalabhati* (see chapter 6).

Unconditional Love Meditation

This meditation is on the total acceptance and unconditional love of Mother Earth, allowing her human custodians to act with free will. She understands and accepts with great humility, that all is happening according to God's Plan and that all in this physical illusion is subject to change. She simply beams her Love and allows flux and flow to occur without judgement, in whichever form that may take.

Breathe into your tail bone and flow your roots down into the glowing light at the heart of the Earth.

Link with the beautiful, maternal energy of the Earth, bask in her love.

Expand and blossom under the deep compassion of the Earth.

Flow upward through your roots into the base of the spine.

Visualise the spine as a golden tube of light (*sushumna*), permeated with the colours of the chakras.

Fill each chakra in turn with the compassion of the Earth: the base chakra, the sacral chakra, the navel chakra, the heart chakra.

Rotate the throat chakra (*vishuddhi)* 90° to face upwards in the golden column of the spine.

Beam that compassion of the Earth into the head and beyond.

Rotate the heart chakra (*anahata*) 90° upwards in the spine.

Observe as both chakras become crystalline and transparent: spiritually charged.

Rotate the throat chakra down towards the heart in the column of the spine.

Beam the golden light of compassion between the two chakras.

Sit within these two centres and bask in the light.

These open the pink Chakra of Unconditional Love in the upper chest.

Bask in the silence and the glory of Unconditional Love.

Feel that Love expanding to the whole of humanity and the whole of creation.

Bask in the Silence and listen.

Feel the expansion of Love for all that is.

Love God.

Listen and be totally conscious for as long as you can.

Feel the flow of *prana* as a light wind through the spine. Sit within this shaft of light.

To return, rotate the petals of the chakras to their outward position in the pit of the throat and the centre of the chest.

Come to physical awareness slowly.

Prayer

Divine Mother, release me from Thy cosmic illusion of separateness.
Awaken with me Love as the only reality.

Chapter 26

Absence of Pride (*na atimanita*)

When a person responds to the joys and sorrows of others as if they were his own, he has attained the highest state of spiritual union. (From *The Bhagavad Gita,* 6:32 translated by Eknath Easwaran, founder of the Blue Mountain Center of Meditation, copyright 1985, 2007; reprinted by permission of Nilgiri Press)

And so we come full circle in the fullness of experience. With spiritual awakening comes humility, as the ego, in all its many guises, eventually falls quiet. All meandering and false routes are revealed before we can be lured by their bright baubles. Intuition, the voice of wisdom and inner knowing, guides us as surely and constantly as the North Star, to the most sacred hallowed ground within: the unwavering, ever-enduring God-flame in our heart cave.

In the beginning, God dreamed the whole of creation in terms of ideas. He said, 'Let there be light: and there was light' (Genesis 1:3). He vibrated dream light into a dream cosmos. Into that astral cosmos, He solidified the dream physical realm.

Our path as a spiritual climber is to retrace creation and to dissolve all dreams into the One Spirit. St Teresa of Avila spent twenty years as a nun struggling with her Catholic faith before breaking free into pure Oneness of Spirit. She wrote some of the most beautiful prayer poems expressing quenchless thirst in Divine Bliss and Love.

Christ has no body now on earth but yours,
No hands but yours,
No feet but yours.
Yours are the eyes through which He is to look out

Christ's Compassion to the world; Yours are the feet with which He is to go about doing good; Yours are the hands with which He is to bless men now.

(*You are Christ's Hands,* St Teresa of Avila from *God Makes The Rivers To Flow: Sacred Literature of the World Selected* by Eknath Easwaran, founder of the Blue Mountain Center of Meditation, copyright 1991, 2008; reprinted by permission of Nilgiri Press, P. O. Box 256, Tomales, CA 94971, www.bmcm. org)

And here we stand on the brink of a holy, new depth of experience of God. Here we move into a heart-opening bliss of surrender from who we believed ourselves to be. Ordinarily, we think of 'myself' as the ego-self but in meditation we learn to unite the ego-consciousness with the intuitive consciousness of the soul. Then the true 'Myself' becomes known. That is why God urges us to lift our eyes from the physical senses and to become absorbed through devotion on the inner 'Myself' or God.

In this chapter, we will be chanting AUM to loosen ties to the physical body, and mentally chanting AUM to loosen ties to form as bound by the astral body. We will be meditating on loosening strings of attachment to outcome and exposing deep-seated ego-driven attachments and expectations. Finally, we will be handing over control of soul expression through eyes, hands and feet to God, so that the blissful formlessness of heaven may be brought in to spiritualise the earth, our role here, and to bless our body-temple.

Pranayama with Aum Chanting

Bring the breath into awareness: the soft inhale and exhale.

Focus on the physical sensation of the breath as perceived through the bridge of the nose.

Is it the inhale or the exhale where you have most awareness of the bridge of the nose?

Perceive that the breath is merely arriving at the bridge of the nose; and then leaving.

Let the physical and energetic awareness at the bridge of the nose fill your entire experience. As if the bridge of the nose was a universe in its own right. Here the breath merely flows through without disturbing the expanding stillness.

Experience of the physical breath is replaced with 'other than breath': an energetic fullness or expanded awareness.

Now chant AUM aloud, retaining focus on the bridge of the nose;

The bones of the face and head.

Then, the whole skeleton as a bony conductor of resonance.

Continue chanting aloud until the bones of the physical body are vibrating.

Ask yourself: what do I have to let go of? Allow that release as you chant AUM.

Visualise vibrating and releasing old patterns (*samskaras*) and stuck emotions.

Release attachment to the physical form.

Next, map your awareness out into the astral field, as a sphere of vibrating light, around you. Chant AUM mentally from the centre of your being. Are you chanting with the exhale? Explore mentally chanting AUM into the pauses in the breath.

Affirm to yourself: there is nothing that I need to do, except let go. Each mental chant of AUM loosens the attachment of the astral realm.

Ask yourself: what do I have to let go of at this level? Imagine that you are attached to a kite which is tugging in the wind, longing to be free. Perhaps this represents a person or a place. Realise that you are holding the string and that in holding the kite back from being free, you are also restricting your own growth.

Take a deep breath in and let the kite go.

Feel how freeing this is.

Imagine that you are holding on to a thousand kite strings of connections.

Take a deep breath in and let them all fly free.

Notice how free and light as air you feel.

Let your awareness be on the expanded astral sphere.

Sit calmly in the very centre.

Any flicker of thought would move you from the centre: realise all thoughts as unreal.

Retain attention in the quiet epicentre of the astral sphere.

Duration: 20-30 minutes.

Meditation on Renunciation of ego-self

Breathe in. Breathe out and offer your eyes to let God's Wisdom be expressed through you. Step back from ownership of your eyes and let go.

Breathe in. Breathe out and offer your hands to let God's Love and Compassion become expressed. Your hands are the instruments of Divine Plan. Withdraw, internally from occupying space within the hands in the body.

How might God extend Love and Compassion through your body as an instrument?

Breathe in. Breathe out and offer your feet to let God's Blessing be expressed through your footprints.

Pan back in this lifetime to all your childhood footsteps. From your very first step, to playing in a garden, the park, the school playground ... let go and spiritualise all your infant steps with God's Love.

See all your footsteps glowing with an imprint of golden light. Those places where you played become golden in the light of God's Blessing through your many footsteps.

Let go of attachment to time or place. See all your footsteps from any lifetime as having left a tracery of golden blessings in your wake. Wherever you have walked, so has God walked within you, expressing the highest divinity through your feet.

Pan back into the astral sphere.

See the physical body within it.

Zoom in closer to the very cells of the physical body pulsing with light.

Look closer into the nucleus of a cell: DNA mapped in a tight double helix spiral within it.

Along the strings of DNA, are 'switches' for specific traits, either on or off.

Switch off all the negative genetic traits.

Charge the cell with photons of light until it burns so brightly it spills over into its neighbouring cells, spiritualising each one.

Pan back in focus to the physical body as it is charged with spiritual light from each cell.

Know that through this spiritual awakening of body, mind and soul, you are charged with God's role for you on this Earth.

Step forward into the centre of your being and let go. Let's God's Love, Light and Compassion be expressed through every step.

Prayer

Divine Father, fill my footprints with your Love. Bless each being through my feet wherever I may tread, as that You may walk through me, lightly upon this Earth. Help me to remember to walk conscious of Your presence and imbuing each step with Your Love.

Part 4

Transcendence through Devotion

The man who is full of faith, who is devoted to it, and who has subdued the senses and obtains this knowledge and having obtained knowledge he goes at once to the Supreme Peace.
(Bhagavad Gita 4:39)

As finally, layer upon layer of illusion is removed, we can at last know that there is only God.

For all followers of the Divine Scent arising intoxicatingly from within, true vision and understanding comes for it is written that he who seeks shall find. The door to soul-freedom is within the heart, where God eternally waits to reveal each ever-new, ever-sweet revelation of all that is.

Meditation on a personal aspect of God as the Heavenly Father, Divine Mother or The Beloved, will unfold from within through love. Love is the key that opens that inner door to God. Intense devotional love is the path to the Interior Castle wherein resides God.

My devotees come unto Me.
(Bhagavad Gita 7:23)

So, let that love whisper along all the fibres of your being, from each chakra, leading in gossamer threads to the thousand petals of *sahasrara* (crown chakra). Know that nothing is beyond your reach. Hitherto, worldly distractions had you engrossed in looking outward until you consciously withdrew from desire for each avenue of distraction, from fear and attachment to outcomes. God alone sustains and nourishes our very soul. God is all there is. In mistakenly trying to seek independence and separateness, we cut ourselves off from Heavenly Peace within.

Man is made in the image of God's love, and by manifesting unconditional love, he can again become like the Father, merging in Him and dropping his acquired second nature as a mortal being. (Paramahansa Yogananda, *God Talks with Arjuna: The Bhagavad Gita* p. 1075)

Pranayama: So Ham breath

'So Ham' is a Hindu mantra meaning 'He I am'. Having no restriction on the breath, allow a mental mantra of *'so'* on the inhale and *'ham'* on the exhale.

Imagine a full moon reflected on the surface of a deep pool of water. Any raggedness of breath or mental focus will distort the reflection into a thousand images of the moon.

Softly breathing, using the mantra, pour your soft *'so ham'* upon the water so as to leave no ripple.

Continue by pouring your heart's devotion through *'so ham'* upon the water.

Dissolve the physical until only the breath exists.

Realise that you are breathing subtle *prana* behind the breath.

Experience your essence flowing through your heart, becoming the watery depths, the silvery reflection and the moon itself.

Devotional Meditation on the Lotus Feet of the Divine Mother

Let the breath become so soft as to be reverential, fanning your devotion over the feet of the Divine Mother.

Be as the Mother's love fanning Her feet with the devotion of the breath.

Imagine the soles of the Divine Mother exposed in recline or in the lotus posture (cross-legged, soles facing upward) as you pour your sweetest love, like an unguent on Her feet.

In the soles of Her feet opens a blue lotus flower, eternally unfolding and unfolding, layer upon layer, perpetually revealing the patterning within creation.

Realise that your small spark is written within the patterning of creation, forever being revealed lotus within the feet of the Divine Mother.

The whole of creation is revealed upon those ever-unfolding, ever-new bliss-filled feet.

Let the edges of the small self lovingly fall within the ever-unfolding, perpetually new creation within the Divine Mother.

All form is continually being brought into creation, expanding and then dissolving into potentials before being re-created and re-expanded. Let the edges of the ego-knowing small-self fall back into the melting pot of Creation within the Mother's Lotus Feet.

Let go into the formlessness blue of all potentials.

Devotional Poem

Sink down into the very depths – there I Am.
Reach to the highest skies – here I Am.
To the infinite realms and wonders of unfolding universes – I Am.
There is no where that I am not.
All souls reside within Me, Ever new and in Bliss
Though some souls slumber in ignorance
And dream of mortality,
Until upon waking into the Wonder of Me,
Find the reality of Love, wrapping and unfolding perpetually,
As a torus of form into formlessness, over and over into infinity.
All forms arise in my dreams of Creation,
A reality which every soul as a God-seed of my Spirit awakens to
By one part spiritual striving and devotion to Me,
A second part, the aid of an illumined master,
And the largest part, an out-pouring of My Grace in answer to
souls' heart-love for Me upon the Water of Souls.
To be asleep is to sink beneath the water surface, perceiving only
murky depths.
In striving for Me, a soul surfaces to find tranquil, peace-embalmed
waters reflecting the Light of My Omnipresence,
Freeing from the pull of surface lure of the waters of slumber, by
soul-longing to be free,
The soul wings homeward in Me.
Inexorably following my intoxicating perfume of Bliss in the
embalming fluid of the out-flowing breath,
My devotee attains God-realisation,
Through My Grace.
(Jenny Light)

Epilogue

In ever-deepening God-consciousness, I find my eyes of the soul wide open in wonder. I have been in this incarnation for over 50 years but only now am I starting to have an inkling as to what it's all about and how little I know. In incredulity, I ask myself: what have I been doing all these years? Sometimes I had felt lost without a guidebook in this strange planet Earth but now the blinkers are removed from my eyes through constant prayer and meditation. I did not come to this depth and slowing down of consciousness on my own. Every step has been guided, although oft times I knew it not.

Persistent prayer has revealed a Deep Peace hitherto unknown in all the alleys of my searching, a hair's breadth from my sight, hidden just under my nose and overlooked. And so sweetly God exudes an all-pervasive divine nectar. Like the musk deer that is driven mad searching for its own intoxicating perfume that it can never find, as I become still, I find that perfume exudes from my inner core, blissfully sweet and ever-renewing in every moment.

And I am filled with humility, for I know that I didn't get here alone but through God's Love and blessed intervention to lead my wandering soul back to its inner core. In the centre of a maze of my own making, is revealed the One I have been searching for! Literally under my nose and no further away than my breath! Down how many countless pathways have I wandered? But by the hand of God, I am restored as One and I realise how little I know. It is only by Divine mercy that the path through the maze alights in golden glory and I know I am home. I have always been home. There is no other home than home in God. You have heard me, Divine Father, as the prayer voice of one crying in the wilderness of existence! And I am humbled that you have heeded my cry.

I stand straight and tall for I know you have blessed me with Thy presence and not found me wanting. All the many pathways of being that I could have dreamed up, I sought to hide from You in shame for all I have done.

I am blessed and all the veils which hid you from my sight are no more and there you are in plain sight, hiding from me no more. I want to jump and embrace You whom I find in the sky and the birds, breath and song, earth-walking and in prayer.

Restlessness is ceased. My eyes are steadily gazing from the centre of Our Spirit connectedness. And I am content. Nothing is needed, Father, for you provide for my every need. You offer to fill my voice with words of your choosing. I need think, plan or scheme no more as you send to me, at the right time, what is just and right. And You I trust to catch me if I should fall and direct my very footstep on the blind-folded path of faith. I am yours, oh Lord. And in that simple humility, I am set free.

Acknowledgements

I would like to thank Sri Paramahansa Yogananada, Sri Swami Sivananda, Eknath Eswaran and Jack Hawley for their inspired translations of the Bhagavad Gita. I would like to thank Jack Hawley for his input and advice in shaping this book. I would like to thank Stephen Sturgess for his advice on presenting the devotion to Guru Paramahansa Yogananada throughout this book. I am totally indebted to my dear friend Neil Campbell for his tireless rereading, valued comments and research for this book.

I am grateful for the kind permission to reprint from the following publishers: St. Teresa of Avila, 'The Interior Castle' by permission of Dover Press. 'The Bhagavad Gita: a Walkthrough for Westerners'. Copyright © 2011 by Jack Hawley, Ph.D. Reprinted with permission of New World Library, Novato, CA. www. newworldlibrary.com. Whispers from Eternity by Paramhansa Yogananda (2008, Crystal Clarity Publishers, Nevada City, California). 'The Path' by Mahatma Gandhi from *God Makes The Rivers To Flow*, Sacred Literature of the World Selected by Eknath Easwaran, founder of the Blue Mountain Center of Meditation, copyright 1991, 2008; reprinted by permission of Nilgiri Press, P. O. Box 256, Tomales, CA 94971, www.bmcm. org. The Dhammapada, translated by Eknath Easwaran, founder of the Blue Mountain Center of Meditation, copyright 1985, 2007; reprinted by permission of Nilgiri Press, P. O. Box 256, Tomales, CA 94971. 'The Power of Now'. Copyright © 2004 by Eckhart Tolle. Reprinted with permission of New World Library, Novato, CA. www.newworldlibrary.com. 'Weaving Your Name' by Kabir from God Makes The Rivers To Flow, Sacred Literature of the World Selected by Eknath Easwaran, founder of the Blue Mountain Center of Meditation, copyright 1991, 2008; reprinted by permission of Nilgiri Press, P. O. Box 256, Tomales, CA 94971,

I am deeply grateful to my students and dear friend Anita Neilson for encouraging me to dive deeply in the path of meditation and to write this book.

Finally, I bow deeply in devotion and gratitude to my guru,

Paramahansa Yogananada for his teachings, insights and support in birthing this book of Divine Meditations.

May this book lead you all deeper on the inward path into Divine Oneness and Evernew Bliss.

Inspirational Reading

'Asana Pranayama Mudra Bandha', Swami Satyananda Saraswati, Bihar School of Yoga, 1969

'Autobiography of a Yogi', Paramahansa Yogananda, Self Realization Fellowship 1946

'The Bhagavad Gita- A Walk Through for Westerners', Jack Hawley, New World Library, 2011.

'Bhagavad Gita', Eknath Eswaran, Nilgris Press, 2007.

'Bhagavad Gita', Sri Swami Sivananda, Divine Life Society Publication, 2000.

'Bhagavad Gita: In the Light of Kashmir Shaivism', Swami Lakshmanjoo, Lakshmanjoo Academy, 2015

'God Talks with Arjuna: The Bhagavad Gita', Paramahansa Yogananda, Self-Realization Fellowship, 2009.

'God Makes the Rivers to Flow', Eknath Easwaran, Nilgiri Press, 1982

'Inner Peace: How to be Calmly Active and Actively Calm', Paramahansa Yogananda, Self-Realization Fellowship, 1999

'Prana and Paranayama', Swami Niranjanananda Saraswati, Yoga Publications Trust, 2009.

"Silent Teaching: The Life of Dom John Main" Paul T. Harris, Spirituality Today, Vol.40 No. 4, pp. 320-32

'Sivastotravali of Utpaladeva: a Mystical Hymn of Kashmir', Swami Lakshmanjoo, D.K.Printworld Ltd, 2008

The Complete Works of the Swami Vivekananda, Volume 1 ,Swami Vivekananda, 1915

'The End of Sorrow: The Bhagavad Gita for Daily Living (Vol 1)', Eknath Easwaran, 1993

The Miracle of Mindfulness, Thich Nhat Hanh, 1975, Beacon Press, Boston, Massachusetts

'The Yoga of the Bhagavad Gita', Parmahansa Yogananda, Self-Realization Fellowship, 2007

'*Whispers from Eternity*', Paramahansa Yogananda, Crystal Clarity Publishers, 2008.'*Prana and Pranayama*', Saraswati Swami Niranjanananada, Yoga Publications Trust, 2009

'*The Power of Now : A Guide to Spiritual Enlightenment*', Eckhart, Tolle, New World Library, 1997

'*The Dhamma-pada*', translation by Eknath Easwaran, Nilgiri Press, 1985

'*The Book of Chakras and Subtle Bodies*', Sturgess, S. Watkins, 2014

'*The Bhagavad Gita: God talks with Arjuna*', Paramahansa Yogananda, Self-Realization Fellowship1995.

'*Interior Castle*', St Teresa of Avila, Dover Press, 1946

'*In the Sanctuary of the Soul*', Paramahansa Yogananda, 1998, Self-Realization Fellowship

MANTRA BOOKS
EASTERN RELIGION & PHILOSOPHY

We publish books on Eastern religions and philosophies. Books that aim to inform and explore the various traditions that began in the East and have migrated West.

If you have enjoyed this book, why not tell other readers by posting a review on your preferred book site. Recent bestsellers from MANTRA BOOKS are:

The Way Things Are
A Living Approach to Buddhism
Lama Ole Nydahl
An introduction to the teachings of the Buddha, and how to make use of these teachings in everyday life.
Paperback: 978-1-84694-042-2 ebook: 978-1-78099-845-9

Back to the Truth
5000 Years of Advaita
Dennis Waite
A demystifying guide to Advaita for both those new to, and those familiar with this ancient, non-dualist philosophy from India.
Paperback: 978-1-90504-761-1 ebook: 978-184694-624-0

In the Light of Meditation
Mike George
A comprehensive introduction to the practice of meditation and the spiritual principles behind it. A 10 lesson meditation programme with CD and internet support.
Paperback: 978-1-90381-661-5

The Less Dust the More Trust
Participating in The Shamatha Project, Meditation and Science
Adeline van Waning, MD PhD
The inside-story of a woman participating in frontline meditation research, exploring the interfaces of mind-practice, science and psychology.
Paperback: 978-1-78099-948-7 ebook: 978-1-78279-657-2

I Know How To Live, I Know How To Die
The Teachings of Dadi Janki: A warm, radical, and life-affirming view of who we are, where we come from, and what time is calling us to do
Neville Hodgkinson
Life and death are explored in the context of frontier science and deep soul awareness.
Paperback: 978-1-78535-013-9 ebook: 978-1-78535-014-6

Living Jainism
An Ethical Science
Aidan Rankin, Kanti V. Mardia
A radical new perspective on science rooted in intuitive awareness and deductive reasoning.
Paperback: 978-1-78099-912-8 ebook: 978-1-78099-911-1

A Path of Joy
Popping into Freedom
Paramananda Ishaya
A simple and joyful path to spiritual enlightenment.
Paperback: 978-1-78279-323-6 ebook: 978-1-78279-322-9

Ordinary Women, Extraordinary Wisdom
The Feminine Face of Awakening
Rita Marie Robinson
A collection of intimate conversations with female spiritual
teachers who live like ordinary women, but are engaged with their
true natures.
Paperback: 978-1-84694-068-2 ebook: 978-1-78099-908-1

Shinto: A celebration of Life
Aidan Rankin
Introducing a gentle but powerful spiritual pathway reconnecting
humanity with Great Nature and affirming all aspects of life.
Paperback: 978-1-84694-438-3 ebook: 978-1-84694-738-4

The Way of Nothing
Nothing in the Way
Paramananda Ishaya
A fresh and light-hearted exploration of the amazing reality of
nothingness.
Paperback: 978-1-78279-307-6 ebook: 978-1-78099-840-4

Readers of ebooks can buy or view any of these bestsellers by clicking on the live link in the title. Most titles are published in paperback and as an ebook. Paperbacks are available in traditional bookshops. Both print and ebook formats are available online.

Find more titles and sign up to our readers' newsletter at http://www.johnhuntpublishing.com/mind-body-spirit. Follow us on Facebook at https://www.facebook.com/OBooks and Twitter at https://twitter.com/obooks.